GH avisualagency™

Design by GH avisualagency™

Introduction by John Robinson
Essay by Helen Walters
Captions by Helen Walters

GH avisualagency™ is a collective of five individuals who work in the area where art and design overlap. Starting out as Graphic Havoc in 1994, the agency has consistently explored the collaborative process and brought an artistic slant to commercial projects and designs for clients such as adidas, Cartoon Network, Warp Records, Coca-Cola and L.A.M.B. Work in all media and styles is featured, with images and descriptions of each project, and collaborative and individual artworks.

Booth-Clibborn Editions

GH
avisualagency™

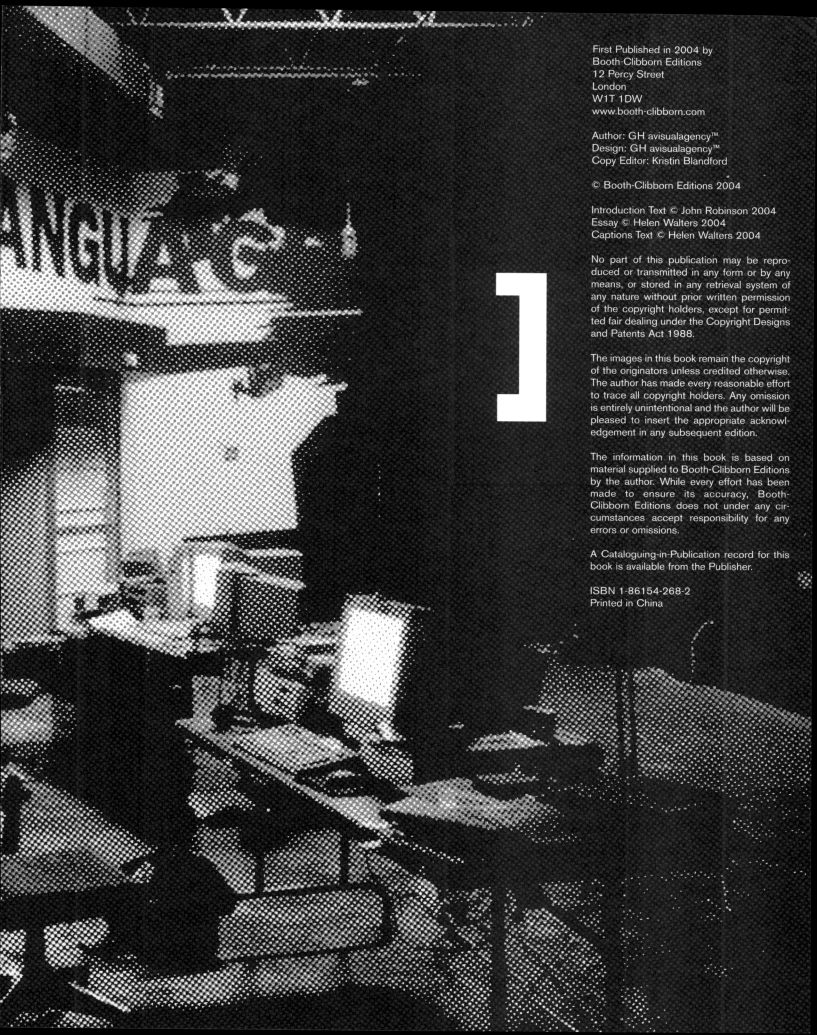

First Published in 2004 by
Booth-Clibborn Editions
12 Percy Street
London
W1T 1DW
www.booth-clibborn.com

Author: GH avisualagency™
Design: GH avisualagency™
Copy Editor: Kristin Blandford

ISBN 1-86154-268-2
Printed in China

Contents:

Graphic Havoc
John Robinson

For the first few years that I was acquainted with Derek Lerner I was sure that he hated me. Later on it turned out that he was just incredibly shy. This was around 1991 in Atlanta and we were in our early 20s. I was making feeble attempts at political graffiti by plastering the word 'INC.' anywhere I could and self-righteously scrawling the secrets of the Freemasons to the captive audience of the toilet stall. I was in college for literature and working at a hipster burrito joint called Tortillas, where I linked up with the first graff writer I ever met: ROME. I started following him and another writer, ION, on bombing missions and all-nighters at legendary Atlanta graffiti yards (Civic and 40), scribbling and experimenting in unused corners while becoming increasingly interested in their varying techniques to produce throw-ups and pieces.

It was all very urban and exciting, and little by little I became more involved with local graff culture. Despite having absolutely no artistic talent, I managed to come up with a semi-respectable tag: GNOSIS (a name that stuck when I discovered that my talent at DJing was far more promising than in any type of visual art). ROME, ION and I formed a crew called BTS ("Beat The System", "Blow The Smoke") and our first beef with another crew (really a joke, in retrospect) was with two locals, ESTRO and MUERTE, who had gone over a wall we had broken in. MUERTE was a scruffy, dreadlocked kid whose name was Scott Herren while ESTRO was a kid known as Goofy to some and as Peter Rentz to his mom. We all wound up becoming close friends and it was they who introduced us to the (in our minds) omnipresent and intimidatingly talented crew known as Graphic Havoc.

This was an amazing time in Atlanta: we were learning about the past while building our own future. Pete and I organized a party called Dub Aquarium in his loft (before the city became riddled with pricey pseudo-lofts) and served bananas and espresso. Musicians, writers, artists, and DJs who knew each other only peripherally began to meet more regularly and formally. Later, in the same loft, Pete rented a 16mm print of *Style Wars* from the public library (before it was available on VHS) and seemingly every writer in the city was there. This was the time that Yin Yang Café opened and artists like Little Jon and the Chronicle, India Arie, and Donny were coming up, starting a new legacy of neo-soul.

Then Atlanta's most famous underground club, MJQ, opened and served as a hub for all of us to drink, listen to good music, and inspire each other. Pete would play on Thursdays with Taka, and I would play Tuesdays and Saturdays with J. Lvcevich. Scott Herren was now better known as DelaRosa and Asora (but not yet Prefuse73 or Savath & Savalas) and worked the bar with SMAZE (who later went on to be a part of Beneath Autumn Sky.) Sadek Bazaraa and I would go record shopping sometimes and chat endlessly in the DJ booth about trip-hop,

jungle, and other exciting new music. I was also working at a video store called Movies Worth Seeing that served as another central social hub for us all. David Merten would come in and chat about movies and was the first person I knew ever to actually purchase a DVD. He was sophisticated and knowledgeable, but when he showed up at MJQ, you knew things were going to get out of control. Meanwhile, over at the bar area, sketch books were being passed around, ideas compared and plans made. It seems fitting then, that MJQ and Graphic Havoc now celebrate their 10-year anniversaries at the same time, since both were the brainchildren of some of the most forward-thinking cats in the city.

At this time and until they left for New York, Graphic Havoc were THE folks you wanted to do your flyers. It's pretty safe to say that not only did they raise the bar for promotional design sophistication in Atlanta, but they also defined a new look and feel to represent what people were doing musically. Actually, make that several new looks and feels: from Randall Lane's striking pylons and warning sticker motifs to Derek's multi-colored graff meets collage style to Pete's line art tennis obsession phase (for example). Regardless of who was working in whatever style they were interested in at the time, Graphic Havoc had less of what you could call a "look" and more of a recognizability factor granted by their consistent innovation and the creative sophistication that set them apart from other designers in Atlanta. God knows I got a lot more crowds out to events because they so capably visually distinguished my crew, Team Rollers, from the other DJ crews out there.

In the mid to late 1990s, as writers started becoming designers and gallery artists, the usual dialogue about what constitutes "selling-out" ensued and clung to the maturing of our generation, as it probably has with all others. As a still-cynical young purist, for me it was more about the question, "what is the intrinsic value of 'good design' anyways?" Thanks to their patience, what I learned from all of the Graphic Havoc guys is that good design has long been a mark of individual and collective craftsmanship that simply evolved from the artisans of the pre-industrial era to the age of mass-production. Chrome work on cars from the 50s may have been seen as mass-produced droll at the time, but the wild, futuristic imaginations of some of those designers is overwhelming now. The same continues in the post-industrial age. Among thousands of television channels, tons of throwaway products and terabytes of useless information online, one can still find the odd jewel of innovative design. Only time will separate the biters from the originators of our generation, but I am perfectly certain that the legacy and influence of Graphic Havoc will live on to inspire future generations.

John "Gnosis" Robinson: Atlanta, GA, 2004

GH avisualagency™
Helen Walters

You might think that being given the opportunity to publish a 228-page book (full color, two different paper stocks) would be any designer's dream. No unreasonable client demands. No 'it's great but could you just make the logo a bit bigger?' No 'can you do it just like that other job you did eight years ago?' On the contrary, here, at last, is total freedom. And indeed, all five partners of GH avisualagency™ were obviously thrilled by the opportunity this book presented. It's just that didn't stop them from worrying about what to put in it or how best to produce it.

In the end, the book's structure is more telling than they perhaps even suspected. Divided into two distinct chapters, one showing off their projects for clients, the other their more personal artworks, their concern to represent themselves in an honest and thoughtful way superceded their desire to stun a reader with displays of graphic trickery or typographic virtuosity. Or, as partner Peter Rentz puts it: "We really wanted to avoid doing one of those self-indulgent, masturbatory design monographs." He adds a little sheepishly, "Though I guess that's what we've made all the same."

This, in a nutshell, neatly sums up *GH's* relationship with the design industry at large. On the one hand, the partners are simply a part of the newest generation of designers to rise through the ranks, ready to love the industry, respect its past, debate, discuss and forge its bright new future. On the other, they are representative of a small but forceful group of designers who want absolutely nothing to do with any 'industry' and who are slightly appalled at even the idea of being part of an establishment. Happily working across all media and stubbornly refusing to accept any prescribed limitations or boundaries, they are knowledgeable and entirely obsessive about design. Nonetheless, they remain resolutely un-starry-eyed and unromantic about its place within and importance to the world at large. They are, in short, the biggest threat the industry has had to face in decades, a Trojan horse within the assembled ranks, primed and ready to burst forth at any moment and delightedly upset the status quo.

Perhaps it will come as no surprise to discover that none of the five members ever formally studied graphic design. Three of them (Randall Lane, Derek Lerner and David Merten) went to the Atlanta College of Art to study drawing, painting, digital video and printmaking. Peter Rentz and Sadek Bazaraa, meanwhile, both have backgrounds in engineering and science, though they met while studying industrial design across town at Georgia Tech.

"The idea of being formally trained as a graphic designer did not appeal to me in the slightest," says Lerner forcefully. "I saw the work that was coming out of that department at ACA at the time and it was so boring. It was brochure designs for restaurants, not done in any kind of interesting way." Lane adds succinctly: "It was stale 80s graphic design. It was horrible."

Instead, all five concentrated on extra-curricular activities, getting involved in the graffiti/skateboarding/music scenes in Atlanta. And though Bazaraa candidly admits that he never quite got to grips with using either spray cans or markers, it's impossible to ignore the obvious impact graffiti has had on their work as a whole. Indeed their very name stems from that of the graffiti crew founded by Lerner and Lane in the early 1990s, Graphic Havoc Artists. "That name actually came from right before I moved from Jacksonville, Florida to Atlanta," says Lerner. "There was this weird, sudden boom of graffiti and the city was like, 'we have to put a stop to this'. The newspaper ran this story saying that they were banning the sale of aerosols to people under the age of 18 in an attempt to stop kids wreaking 'graphic havoc' on the streets."

As such, they christened their design agency Graphic Havoc, dropping the word "Artists" to differentiate their projects for clients from their individual, personal work. Even back then they were very well aware of the tension and differences between art and design and then, as today, all five deliberately worked on very personal projects entirely apart from their commercial work. As seems only appropriate, these side projects are not purely visual: Los Angeles-based

Rentz, for example, co-runs a record label, Eastern Developments, for which he commissions his own agency to produce artwork. Bazaraa, meanwhile, plays guitar in one of the label's bands, Bear in Heaven.

"For me, fine art and commercial art are two completely different worlds," says Merten. "As such they require two different mindsets. I don't romanticize graphic design any more: it's a job. I mean of course it's fun, you get to be creative, but with a painting you'll stay up all night because you're obsessing over it."

"I'm sure they influence each other," agrees Lane. "But my artwork definitely doesn't look like my design and my design doesn't look like my paintings or sculptures or whatever it is I'm working on at that time."

In 2000, the agency relocated from Atlanta to Brooklyn, with Rentz opening up the LA office in 2002. "We have a lot of pride in Atlanta, we really wanted to stay there and say 'Screw New York! Screw California! There's no reason Atlanta can't be as cool as them!'," says Lane. "And then we realized that actually there was no way that was true. We were living in a one-museum town…"

In 2004 they changed their name to GH avisualagency™. "The word 'havoc' proved to have a bit of a stigma to it," says Lerner of this decision. "It had been catchy, but once the company passed its tenth anniversary, we decided we wanted to show its maturity." In other words, they realized that while havoc might be a pleasing idea in theory (or in personal work), it isn't necessarily what some paying clients are looking for when employing an agency to work on their projects. "We thought it would be more accurate to have our name reflect the fact that we're about good design, not one particular style or market," Lerner continues. "People sometimes assumed that we only did edgy or youth-focused work, and that's just not the case."

But hang on a minute, how on earth did some punk/skate/graffiti kids with a somewhat cavalier attitude towards design and branding – not to mention no knowledge of how actually to run a business – end up celebrating ten years as a design agency? Well this is where the industry should sit up and take note, because as it happens they did it pretty much by soaking it all in and making it up as they went along. Alienated by the quality of teaching on offer in school, the five embraced the traditional punk philosophy of Do-It-Yourself, and did just that. They were helped along the way by a number of crucial discoveries, including magazines such as *Raygun* and *Émigré* and work by the likes of Neville Brody, P. Scott Makela and The Designers Republic.

"As soon as we found out that there were people out there who were doing things that weren't boring restaurant brochures, and that there was actually some amazing graphic design out there, we immediately became more interested in the whole industry," says Lane. "Our design world immediately opened up from being centered around clothing, graffiti, skateboards and club flyers to being a much larger thing."

Inspired by their mentor, former skateboarding professional Andy Howell, Lane and Lerner took their lead from recent start-ups such as Freshjive and Zero Sophisto and started their own clothing line, Theft Clothing Incorporated. Encouraged rather than disheartened when it became clear that people were more interested in their graphics than their clothes, they decided to act decisively. "The main reason we even started Theft was because we liked to design creative things," explains Lane. "When we realized that we were making more money doing design work, and it was less stress than trying to make and sell garments, it was fairly simple to migrate from one to the other."

So Graphic Havoc was born, with Lerner and Lane working from the apartment they shared with fellow designer Mike Hirsch (also a partner in the company for a short time). And though Lane worked first at Kinkos and then at Turner

Broadcasting Systems, Inc., meaning that Lerner was initially the only full-time employee, they slowly built themselves both a reputation and a client list, calling on friends to join them as they got busier (Merten officially joined in 1996, Rentz and Bazaraa in 1997).

All the while, they exploited the facilities of their various schools and employment and continued to try to teach themselves whatever they could, unabashedly calling on friends such as José Gomez, teachers including Peter Wong and sometimes even complete strangers whenever they really needed help. "I clearly remember going to the graphic design studios at ACA and asking this typography teacher if he knew how to get something from screen to print," says Lerner. "He looked over the file and explained the process of four color printing to me. I couldn't tell you what his name was but he did give me the phone number of a printer that we ended up using for a long time after that: Reflections Printing, way the hell out in the middle of nowhere."

As might be expected, the computer provided something of a revelation. Lerner's father bought them a Quadra 650 (which they only retired from service in 2003) after his son persuaded him that doing so would change his life. "Those were my exact words," says Lerner happily. Even so, right from the beginning they saw the computer as just another way to create work. "It was just another tool with which to make things," says Merten. "It wasn't like everything we did was created on the computer, then or now. We used it in addition to our regular painting and drawing, often printing out stuff and then drawing on it or messing around with it in some way."

Meanwhile, across town, Bazaraa and Rentz were experimenting in their own time and in way. "We were pretty frustrated at Tech so I taught myself all the core computer applications: Illustrator, Photoshop, Quark," says Bazaraa. "I started doing album and promo design for the record label Table of The Elements and learned far more than I ever had at school. Having studied engi-

neering for years and years, art and design suddenly 'happened'. Period. I was really inspired and worked my ass off.'

'Peter and long time friend Jennifer Smith started a projection crew called Executive Projects, which soon grew to include myself and another close friend, Bryan Collins," he continues. "I remember Pete and I going on many late night dumpster-diving missions to different service bureaus around town – pulling out slides, films and transparencies. We would cut them up, add Letraset, photocopy on them, anything we could think of. Slowly we built up a huge arsenal of material and started doing projections at parties and clubs around town. It turned into this massive onslaught of graphics, photos, and moving image."

As such, while Rentz in particular seems to regret a lack of formal education in either graphic design or branding, even he argues that in a strange way it's probably helped them to create different looking, unexpected work. "I have to say that I wish I did have a formal graphic design training because I'm sure there are things that I don't know," he says. "But maybe it's good that we don't have formal design training because it reminds us we don't know everything. That constant self-doubt eating away at you is a positive attribute."

For his part, Lerner argues that the process of branding should be based on intuition rather than education. "When I was in junior high school, even before I got into fine art, I was always drawing logos," he says. "When I was in seventh grade I came up with this one design which said DRL Design which I scree printed onto the back of a military field jacket. We started off with Theft, branding it and building it and watching it grow and then we got another client, [clothing boutique] Wish, for which we did pretty much everything for years. We were able to do it, to watch how it happened and then learn from that and allow it to influence us. We live in a world where we are surrounded by branding. If you are a visual person and you take the time to look at it and think about it and try to understand it then you're going to know what's good and what's not good."

And GH's work is really very good. Not always beautiful, it's nonetheless complex and detailed, with layer upon visual layer creating levels of meaning that unfold exponentially. Meanwhile, their level of active collaboration means that while one person might start on a project, the others will add and subtract elements to ensure that the final results could never have come from one person alone. Those results, therefore, are all the more unexpected. (They do, however, admit that this has become less practical as the years have gone by and they've got too busy to work this way all the time). But what's perhaps most surprising of all is the fact that even after all this time they are still taken aback by the ideas and work of their partners.

"When I first met and got to know Peter, I just thought he was into skateboarding and graffiti," says Lerner. "Then someone told me that he had come up with an idea to make a one-handed point and shoot camera that worked like a gun. He showed me all these perfect schematic sketches and it turned out he really had invented a camera!" Merten adds simply: "the way Peter's mind works is still the biggest mystery to me."

Rentz, in turn, professes to being constantly amazed at how his partners in New York approach work. "I feel like I over-think everything while they just solve the problem and make it look really good too. I think I solve the problem but it doesn't look good. That's why I respect them so much." And while they are in constant communication with each other via email and Instant Messenger, it is clear that influences from their very different educations, along with the different cultures of Los Angeles and New York, all feed into and influence their work.

But where they surpass some of their street-inspired peers is that they are very definitely not simply reproducing something for which they have already made a name. Yes, some of their work may have a certain graffiti twist, but there is no one GH look. They are not simply ripping off an existing style or repeating something they have already perfected. "In graffiti, biting or copying someone else's style is very looked down upon," says Rentz. "Design should be about problem solving, and while stylistic trends come and go, if they don't solve a problem then in five years it will look like hell. It's all style and no substance."

Nor do they only work in one medium. This may have confused clients over the years, but it also adds to the sense that while GH will obviously continue to evolve, they're neither stuck in a rut nor done just yet. "We always wanted to do everything," says Lane. "It's why we describe ourselves as 'avisualagency'; we didn't want to do just print or just web or just interiors…. Clients do sometimes have a hard time dealing with that, they want to feel like they completely understand what you do, but we'd be bored to death if we only did one thing."

Their work includes graphics for record sleeves and flyers (Prefuse73, Lush), packaging (Coca-Cola), advertising (Sprite, USA Network), interiors (Wish), web design (adidas, SWAT), corporate identities (ENML™, Soap Box Studios), fashion design (L.A.M.B.), broadcast design (Cartoon Network, MTV), film titles (*Claire*). Oh, and then there are the installations, exhibitions, records, products (etc.) which are the result of their spare time. The fact that they have any spare time is surprising in itself, but this wilful diversity is enough to drive any would-be pigeonholers insane. But, explains Rentz: "You have to grow; if you're not growing you're dead. And if you don't do things twice then at least you're growing."

But so what of the fact that almost despite themselves they are becoming a part of the design establishment and community? Speaking at international conferences, publishing monographs of their work; it seems their admirers shouldn't worry, their radicalism hasn't left them altogether just yet. While obviously excited and happy to be publishing their own book, they're still resolutely unimpressed by their new-found grandeur, poking fun at themselves and simply refusing to take themselves too seriously. In an industry as spectacularly ego-driven as design, that's definitely something worth celebrating.

Miscellaneous
**EVENT FLYERS &
PROMOTIONAL MAILERS**
1994-99

So this is where it all began. Our friend Jamie Ward was the first to ask us to make some flyers for his weekly party, The Beat Motel, and it went from there. Initially, we were working from the kitchen of a one-bedroom apartment on 16th Street in Atlanta, with lots of trips to Kinkos, where Randall worked. The photocopier was undoubtedly the most important tool we had in the early days, not just because we were into experimenting and seeing what we could create

with it, but also because we didn't know the first thing about the printing process.

Thanks to a friendly typography teacher at the Atlanta College of Art, we learned about film and proofs and printing in general and we began to work from our computer, a Macintosh Quadra 650, still regularly using the photocopier to fuck around with images. Stylistically, anything went. We were experimenting with type and

graphics as much as we possibly could, taking inspiration from people we were into, including the usual suspects, Neville Brody, Vaughan Oliver, David Carson and Tomato, mixed up with elements from our own photographs, paintings, illustrations, etc.

As time went on we got a hell of a lot quicker at churning out flyers (often because we had no choice, having only a few hours to design and produce them). They provided a good

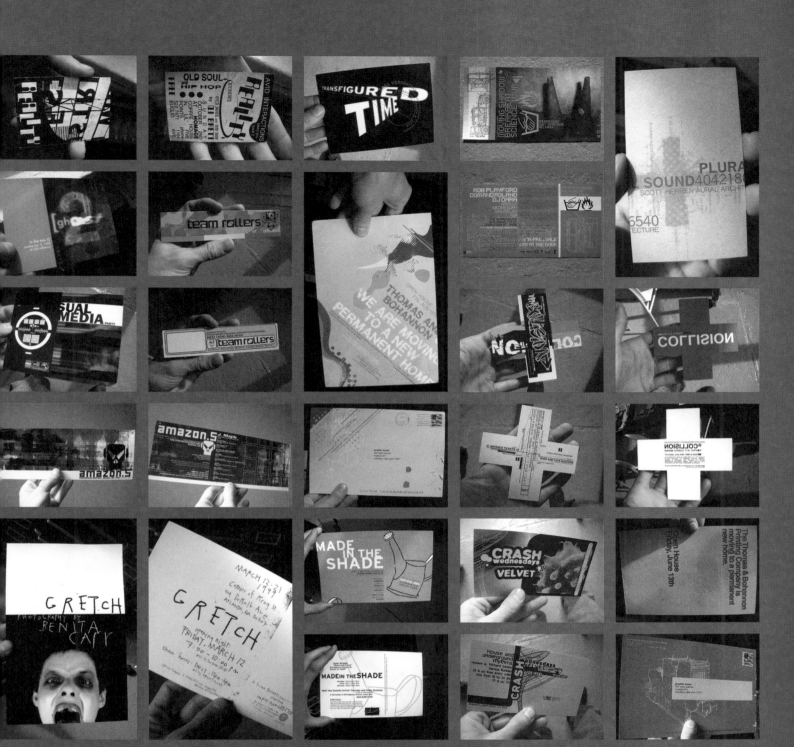

learning experience and they can be fun to do, though they can also be a lot of work for not much money.

We eventually relented and got our stuff printed at A&A Graphics and Printing in Los Angeles. "Relented" because even though A&A offered the best prices and the quickest turn-around time, they also printed roughly 90% of all the club flyers in Atlanta at the time. As a result everything looked and felt the same and we were extremely reluctant for our work to blend in with everyone else's. But once we accepted that there was no alternative and A&A really was the cheapest option, we simply did everything we could to make sure our work stood out from the crowd. One of the most effective ways to ensure this was to endure lots of long-distance arguments with A&A founder, Artie Parent. Ah, the good old days...

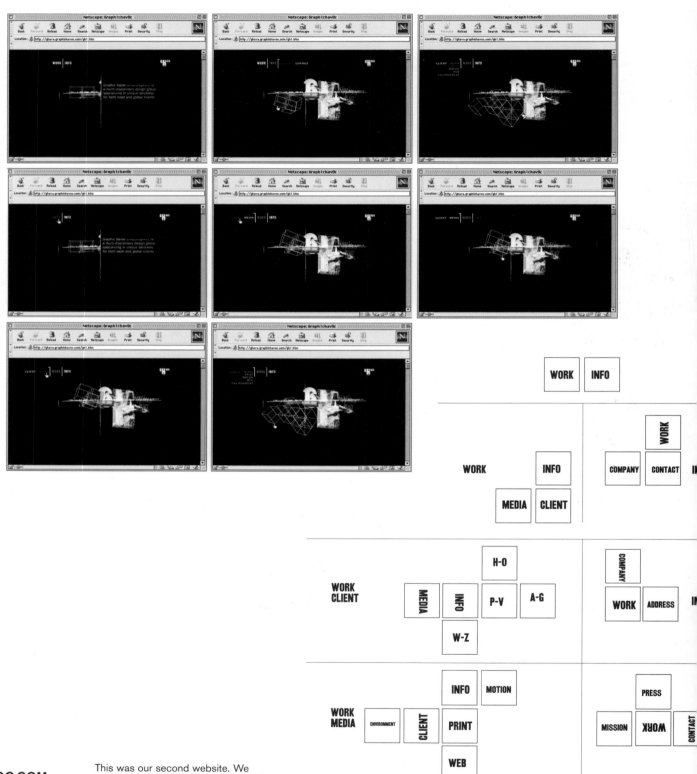

Graphic Havoc
GRAPHICHAVOC.COM
Second launch
1996

This was our second website. We started working on it right when Flash first came out, and it took us forever to finish. We wanted to have a three-dimensional navigation device rather than a series of "pages", which was what most websites consisted of back then. Each cube in the grid represented a different section of the site (past projects, contact details, etc.) and when you clicked on one of its sides, the whole 3-D grid would

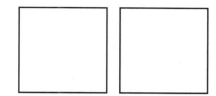

WORK | INFO

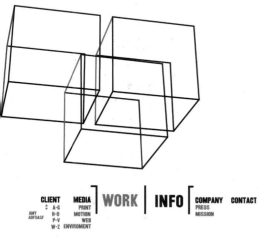

CLIENT   MEDIA   ⌉ **WORK** | **INFO** ⌈ COMPANY   CONTACT
‡ A-G   PRINT   PRESS
AMY   H-O   MOTION   MISSION
ADFSASF   P-V   WEB
           W-Z   ENVIROMENT

FO

rotate to show the relevant details. It was dealing with information in space rather than using a more traditional, linear navigation. It doesn't seem so radical now, but trying to make it work back then was hugely complicated. All the 3-D work had to be done in Adobe Dimensions and exported frame-by-frame, then imported into Flash. It was a bit of a nightmare from start to finish and in the end it turned out to be a bit difficult to navigate, as

well. Oh, and we included far too much content which meant it was painfully slow (this was in the days of 56K modems, before Broadband). But it was very different from what was out there at the time and a real progression from our own first website (which comprised HTML we had coded by hand) so we were proud of it all the same.

Graphic Havoc
SELF-PROMOTIONAL POSTER
1994

This double-sided poster was one of our earliest self-promotional pieces. It was fairly big, with four color process printing on both sides: Artie at A&A printed 1000 of them for us as a thank you for all the work we had put his way.

We had started working on a project called Fax Wars, for which we would fax something to our friend George Estrada, who was working at Modern Dog in Seattle Wa. at the time. He would add to the "art" and fax it back to us. The cross motif you can see here was one of the very first things we had faxed through to him: we were beginning to build up our own personal visual libraries, and certain shapes and forms turn up again and again. Here though, we should also acknowledge the work of British designer Nick Bell. We had seen something he had done which was published in Émigré magazine and this is our "homage" to that piece of work. That basically means that we copied it, but in our own defense we were only young and still very much experimenting with this newly discovered business of "graphic design". It was copying in the best, most respectful way possible.

Graphic Havoc
SELF-PROMOTIONAL PIECES
1994-2004

Right from the beginning we were pretty obsessive about getting our name out there as much as possible. We made stickers that we would slap onto any piece of mail which left the studio (as well as all around town). We were constantly experimenting with different ways of printing, using any materials or methods we could think of. We were also as economical as possible: if there ever happened to be any spare space on a print run, we would use it to produce something for the company. Shown here are a variety of different promos from across the years, including our moving card from Atlanta to Brooklyn (the envelope was two bits of cardboard stuck together with stickers) and the invitation to our New Year's Eve party in 1999, which was a photocopy transfer onto thick card stock.

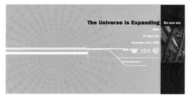

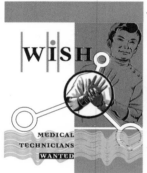

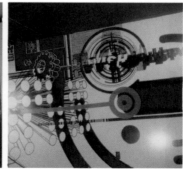

Keywords
ID DEVELOPMENT, MARKETING & PROMOTIONALS, FONTS, ENVIRONMENTAL, LOGO

Concurrent Events
DEREK'S CAR STOLEN, STUDIO RENOVATIONS & NEW FURNITURE, MJQ OPENS

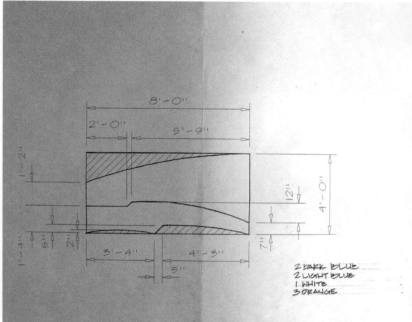

Wish Boutique, Atlanta
WISH
Corporate identity, typeface, T-shirts, promotional materials, instore graphics, environmental design...

Wish was our first major client and we still work with its founder, Louis Ceruzzi. We started out just designing a few T-shirts and flyers, but then somehow we persuaded them to let us work on their corporate identity (the doodle which eventually became their logo is in Derek's sketch book, top left). We had already designed this font, *Droplet*, based on the Holox gas company logo, and it worked really well for them. It was all glow-stick-waving, whistle-blowing, raver-kid stuff and though that wasn't really our scene, we quickly proved that we knew just what was appropriate.

We ended up doing a huge amount of work for Wish, including our first environmental design projects, collaborating directly with various architects on two brand new stores. Scrim walls with cut-out shapes referencing *Droplet* were built to divide the space and a cash-wrap as well as a DJ booth were custom designed for the project. We used photocopied supergraphics, plotter cut vinyl graphics, colored Plexiglas, and lots of orange and blue paint inside the shops. It was pretty wild and unlike anything else in Atlanta at the time.

We should mention the influence of a certain Sheffield-based company here. The Designers Republic is probably the most ripped-off design firm in the world and along with everyone else we were totally influenced by them. Their use of Illustrator was pioneering, and they were the first to capture the way the early 1990s actually felt. We took that and ran with it for this client.

27

Keywords
PHOTOCOPY, BROADCAST, VIDEO, ON-AIR, COMMERCIAL, STOP FRAME ANIMATION

Concurrent Events
PETER BUYS A 72 VOLVO STATION WAGON, *TORTILLAS* BECOMES A ONCE A WEEK LUNCH SPOT

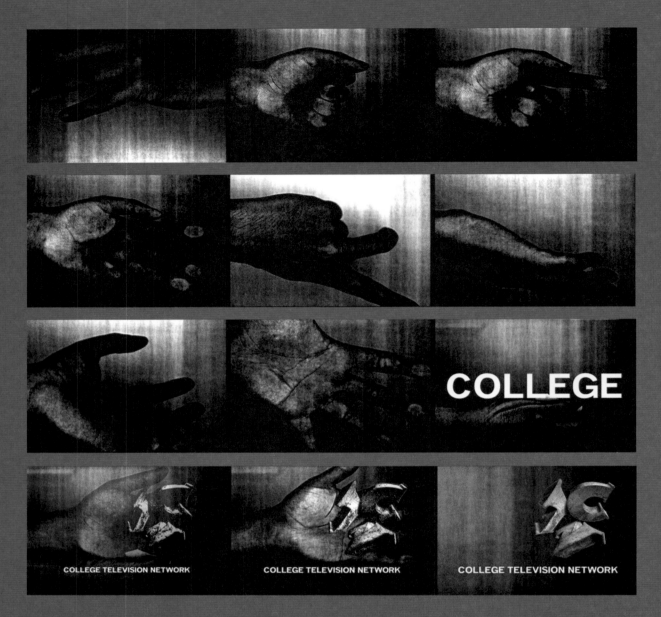

College Television Network
CTN ON-AIR PROMO
1996-1997

The first thing we noticed on taking on this project was that the CTN logo pretty much sucked. The 3-D cluster of type was really hard to make out even at a decent size; if you reduced it too much, it just turned into a blob. So being commissioned to develop a series of four 15-second promotionals presented something of a challenge, to say the least.

Once again, the photocopier provided our salvation and allowed us to design something interesting, which exploited the limited capabilities of the logo. In this case, Randall used a high quality flash photocopier kindly (albeit unknowingly) lent by Turner Broadcasting Systems, Inc., where he had a day job at the time. He placed a cutout of CTN's logo directly onto the scanner and photocopied every single moment of the movement. Then we scanned all of the pages and put them together in AfterEffects to create the animation.

Burrell Communications: Atlanta
COKE BOOK COVER
1998

Lots of people argue that a brand's logo is sacrosanct and should always be left untouched. That's how it always seemed, anyway. So we bore that in mind when we were commissioned by Burrell Communications to create a book jacket design for their client, Coca-Cola. They promptly rejected our beautifully conservative designs, which treated the logo with almost religious respect and instead chose the most experimental design draft presented. This was a good reminder for us not to try and second guess a client or do what other people might do but always to go with our gut instinct.

The books were intended for kids in "urban high schools" and so for the chosen design, we created a multi-layered collage effect based on the existing, everyday urban environment of wheat-pasted, ripped-up, layered and graffitied posters that we felt the students would instantly recognize and relate to. We didn't use much of Coke's traditional iconography, just the bottle shape and some of their existing brand language. In fact, the only obvious logo ends up on the inside cover of the book.

We can safely say that this is the biggest job we have ever worked on in terms of the quantity of print run: a million book covers were printed. We were given three (not that we're bitter, of course).

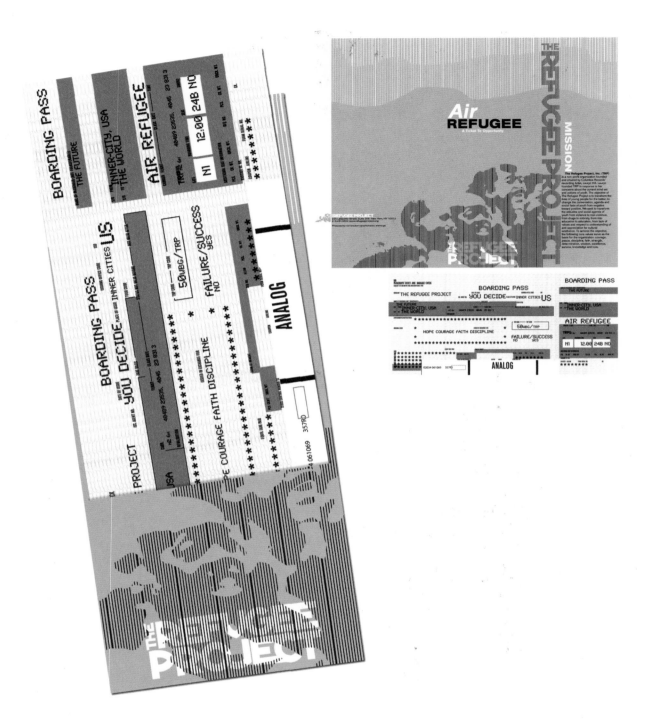

Nomenudum

THE REFUGEE PROJECT

Trifold brochure
1998

Singer Lauryn Hill, formerly of the band The Fugees, founded The Refugee Project with the aim to give kids from under-privileged areas the chance to get away from home for a break. We were commissioned to come up with a promotional brochure for the program (actually more of a two-sided flyer which folded into three) and we decided it made sense to use an airline ticket as an integral part of the design.

We were supplied with photography which we enlarged and filled in with a pattern and then the tickets slipped into a slit cut into the middle of the back cover. Admittedly the ticket thing was a little gimmicky, but it seemed appropriate and it gave us the excuse to print in two colors. Many people seem to revel in printing in full color, but for some reason we've always had a bit of a thing for two-color printing.

Keywords
ID DEVELOPMENT, FLASH, ILLUSTRATION, ANIMATION, INTERNET BUBBLE ABOUT TO BURST

Concurrent Events
GH CONSUMES LOTS OF AURORA COFFEE & MAKES FUN OF DAVE MATTHEWS BAND

zapzoom, Inc.
ZAPZOOM.COM
Identity, font, website
1998

Zapzoom.com was going to be a data collection portal, gathering all sorts of information on youth markets and what kids were into. It was a really hot thing at the time; in fact, it felt like all anyone could talk about was trend forecasting or youth culture and all that kind of bullshit.

Anyway, the company's founder, Todd Triplett, commissioned us to create an identity for the company so he could

go and get venture capital investment for it. We based the look and feel on comic books, notably Sam Kieth's *The Maxx* series, and then later on we created some hugely elaborate, quite weird-looking Flash animations which were hand-drawn and then scanned in and streamlined to make a layered, 3D effect. Sadly, they haven't really been seen: the internet bubble burst shortly after we made the animations and the whole thing got shelved.

However, it was then that Randall uttered the immortal words, "let's do a fully animated music video". Somehow we persuaded a client that this was a completely feasible idea when it just wasn't. We had to admit that we had made a terrible mistake after about two months, when it became clear that we could work on it for a year without ever completing it. Even though we didn't do it on purpose, we still feel horrible about it now.

31

Ian Vanslyke
LUSH
1997-1998

Lush was a monthly after-hours party that became legendary in Atlanta. Ian Vanslyke commissioned us to design and produce flyers for each event, and we had them all printed business card-size. Not only was this quite unusual, it was also satisfying in that they were a good contrast with the bullshit, enormous, foldout flyers

which people at the time seemed to think were somehow interesting, radical or necessary.

At the beginning, Ian insisted that the type size of their name be huge, so earlier examples are interestingly bad rather than life-changingly brilliant. After a while he came to trust us a bit

more and ended up giving us free rein to do whatever we wanted, so the type size came down and we began to experiment a lot more with graphics, type and images, often using some of David's personal photography as a starting point.

Keywords
LETRASET, ANTONI TAPIES, SPELL CHECK, SHOPLIFTING, Kinkos

Concurrent Events
THE PINK PONY IN ATL. BECOMES GH'S OFFICE AWAY FROM THE OFFICE

Manipulation Records
MANIPULATION COMPILATION SLEEVE
Album packaging
1996

Ok, deep breath. This job provided us with one of the most painful lessons we ever had to learn. We had already designed the logo for this record company, and we were obviously delighted when they commissioned us to design our first record sleeve, for a compilation album of tracks by some of their acts. The background of the design was taken from some index cards we had found in an old print shop's warehouse. They looked just like aging paintings, they were amazing and we were really excited about the design. So far so good, right? Well, yes, but when we sent the files to the printer, we forgot to convert them from RGB to CMYK. One small forgetful moment led to one ruined sleeve, which printed in black and white. Oh, and we managed to misspell both words in the title. The craziest thing of all is that it went through every alleged check without anyone picking up on any of the errors. So this is the very first time that the cover is being seen in all its four-color glory and we'd never like to mention it again. Thank you.

Aki Spicer
[MACHINE]
1999

We first collaborated with Aki Spicer and Anthony Hakmati on an animation project for an exhibition held at Atlanta's Nexus Contemporary Art Center. The show went well, leading to the creation of an art collective called Machine, of which we were an occasional part.

They hired us to come up with an identity for the group and so, taking our cue from the word "machine" we used abstract shapes and lines, digital noise, computer chaos, barcodes and dirty, fucked-up type as the major design elements for what turned out to be a strikingly loose and informal identity system.

This was also our first use of the parenthesis, which promptly turned into a bit of an addiction, cropping up in all sorts of unexpected places throughout our work. Looking back now, other designers were also using random punctuation marks (including arrows and asterisks) so there was obviously something in the air/water.

At the time though, we didn't analyze it too much, we just thought it seemed right and looked good. However, we did eventually put a stop to it before it got completely out of control.

This was also our first chance to over-print silver on black ink onto uncoated, colored French paper. Not many clients are prepared to shell out for specialty printing, but obviously this one understood how powerful it could be and we absolutely took advantage of that fact.

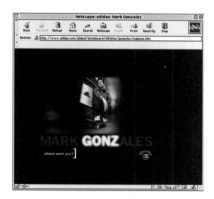

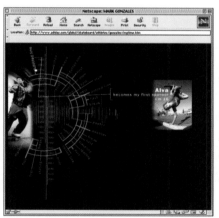 

adidas International Online
ADIDAS.COM/GONZ
Mark Gonzales mini site
1998

Legendary pro-skateboarder Mark Gonzales collaborated with adidas to launch a pair of signature shoes and adidas wanted to let the world know about it – in stages. As such, we initially designed a holding page using close-ups of some of the photography they had supplied to us, announcing "he's coming" without being specific about who was coming or why.

Using that look as our basis, we then developed a content-rich site that told you anything you might ever want to know about Gonzales and his achievements – and then some. We used a non-linear style of navigation: a revolving information wheel with spikes sticking out of it relating to text, photographs or illustrations.

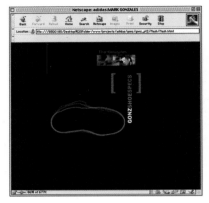

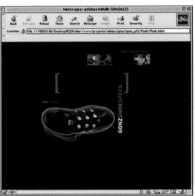

The final part of the Mark Gonzales mini-site featured a discussion between the designer of the shoe and Gonz himself. We took our lead from our previous work on the project and featured the key points from the discussion in a rather neat diagram. The shoe itself was photographed in 360 degrees so users could virtually rotate it.

However, it was at about this time that we realized we were spending far too much time trying to write code and not enough time designing or being creative. Learning code was initially both challenging and interesting, but after a while it ended up simply becoming tedious. From this point on we made a decision to farm out most of our coding to freelancers.

Keywords
BROADCAST, FILM, VIDEO, PROJECTION, TV, COMMERCIAL, ON-AIR

Concurrent Events
EXECUTIVE PROJECTS STARTED, GH'S WAMDUE MUSIC VIDEO IN RESFEST

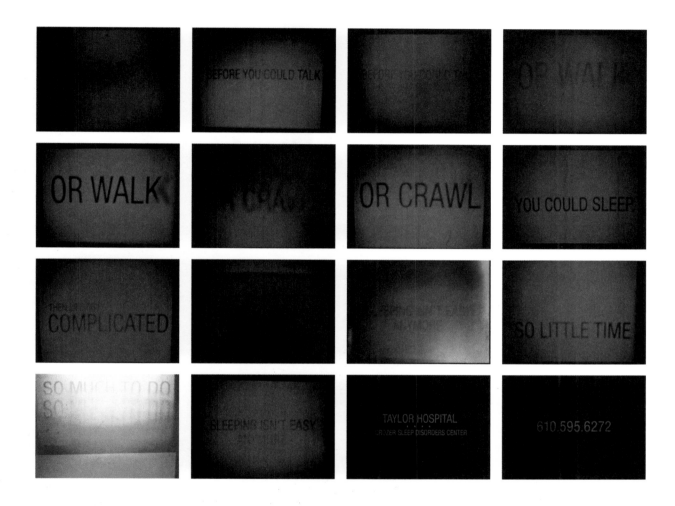

Crozer Sleep Disorder Center

CROZER SLEEP DISORDER CENTER

30-second TV commercial
1998

As you can probably guess from their name, the Crozer Sleep Disorder Center helps people suffering from insomnia. We were commissioned to come up with a "dreamy" ad, using copy supplied to us by the ad agency. We commissioned some audio (from our friend Scott Herren) that featured someone reading out the text and then had various words and parts of sentences float up onto the screen. This was while Peter and Sadek were heavily involved in The Executive Projects and working a lot with transparencies and projections, so we decided to print slides, project them and then shoot the projections using an 8mm film camera. By rolling a glass in front of the projector we created some weird blurs and distortions to give the type a really interesting look. We transferred the film to beta and pumped up the color a bit to give it that rich, soft, deep feeling and then synched it up to the audio. Basically it was a much easier animation job than it would have been if we'd used more typical techniques and it turned out really well, too.

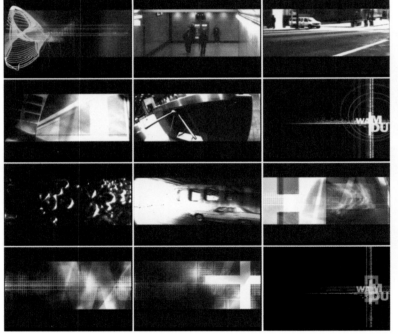

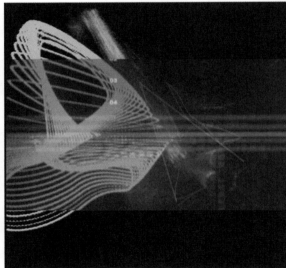

Strictly Rhythm Records
WAMDUE PROJECT
Album packaging, promotional materials, & video projections
1997

Chris Brann is a well-known house musician in Atlanta. We had known him for some time when he asked us to design a record sleeve for his new DJ collective, called Wamdue Project.

We used one of Derek's paintings as our starting point, altering its colors a bit. That became the basis for everything we did later: the album and single sleeves and all the street promotions. It all went really well so Chris asked us to direct and animate some video projections for his live

shows (this thing blew up really fast, he ended up at number one in the UK charts – above Madonna – and he toured all over the world). We had a half hour time allowance so we went around Atlanta using a motor drive on a SLR camera to take lots of still images of Chris and some of his friends. Then we animated the photographs, piled graphics and other footage shot using a DV camera on top, looped all the sequences and generally messed around to create the final piece.

This project was featured in the second Resfest, a festival of motion graphics, music videos, etc. We used the screening as an excuse to come up to New York City. That was when we started thinking seriously about leaving Atlanta. Eventually, in 2000 we moved to Brooklyn.

39

Keywords
"NO LOGO ID DEVELOPMENT", 3D, 2 COLOR, UNCOATED PAPER

Concurrent Events
PETER GETS DOORED & PUNCTURES LUNG, $35G'S LATER...

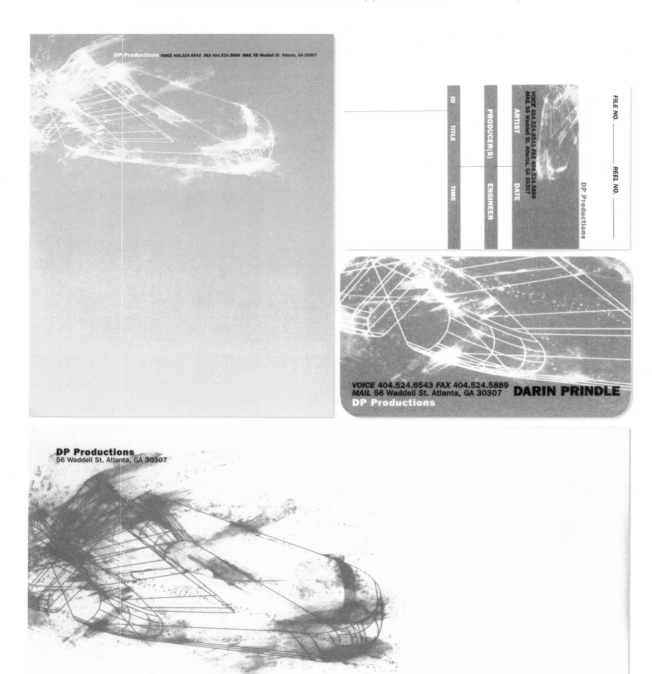

Darin Prindle
DP PRODUCTIONS
Corporate identity system
1998

This was our first job for local Atlanta entrepreneur, Darin Prindle. He was a music engineer/producer and DP Productions was an audio production company, just one of his many ventures.

This was the first time that we created an identity system that wasn't based around the idea of a fixed logo. Instead it was much more organic, with a theme of elements and colors used to create a distinctive look and feel. Peter

made a three dimensional wireframe model of the letters "D" and "P" which Sadek then pretty much destroyed (admittedly that sounds a bit dodgy but we find that if we all contribute to a project then the results are always much more than one person could have imagined). Then we scanned it, arranged and rearranged the resulting images to work out an interesting way of putting all the components together without there ever being one static mark. The background image that you can see

here recurs throughout the whole system (which included video and DAT sleeves, notepads, basically all kinds of collateral materials). Darin was really open to experimentation: he trusted us to get on with the job in hand. The only downside to the system would have been if he had ever needed to "send his logo" to someone, but it wasn't that kind of company so it all worked out just fine.

Anunnaki Entertainment
GAELLE
Album slip-sleeve (one of a series)
1998

Phil Tan of Anunnaki Entertainment commissioned us to come up with a series of EP sleeves and a website for four of his artists, including William of Orange, Wes Yoakam and the solo singer Gaelle. With no photography or anything for us to use, we had to go down more of an abstract route and as a result all of the sleeves ended up looking completely different from each other. We had always been really into P. Scott Makela's work, particularly his work on the *Scream* video for Michael and Janet Jackson so we took that as a starting point for the titles on this cover before going off in our own direction. As usual we seem to have taken it to a darker place, with damaged, dirty type looking like it's floating in space.

The Coca-Cola Corporation
SPRITE
Murals for South American market
1997

Don't laugh, but we actually wore suits to our first meeting with Sprite. What made it even more surreal was that then we had to sit there and listen to their quasi-religious brand talk. We endured two hours of being told about how relevant Sprite was to modern humanity and the importance of its brand philosophy, all supported with elaborate diagrams displayed using an overhead projector. Now we take our work as seriously as the next person, but all that in order to

commission some graphics to go on a wall? The over-thinking that was going on was truly scary but it was an illuminating insight into the world of big business.

Ironically, the brief that they gave us was actually fairly ambiguous, the old "we want something cool but we're not quite sure what" chestnut. The only stipulation was that we had to use their existing "Obey Your Thirst" tagline, so we came up with

a number of different solutions. We're not even sure which were produced in the end but here's a selection of some of the drafts that we came up with, including the ones where we were trying hard to do something we thought they might actually use. Our favorite has to be the one featuring the quote about Grandmaster Flash. Even given the saturation of contemporary culture with references to graffiti and hip-hop, that would still stop you today.

Keywords
ID DEVELOPMENT, PACKAGING, MARKETING, CREATIVE CONSULTING

Concurrent Events
DAVID BUYS ROSARITA (a 1972 Ford 100 short bed truck) & SCARES THE HELL OUT OF ALL OF US

Yvette Petit
SOAPBOX STUDIOS
Corporate identity system
1997

Soapbox Studios was an audio post-production company in Atlanta which turned out to be one of our favorite clients, allowing us to produce even apparently impractical ideas. To create the logo, Derek mixed ink with soap and used a straw to blow bubbles onto a piece of paper. When the bubbles dried, they burst, and once we found the shape we wanted we scanned it in to make the logo, setting it behind Helvetica type. Not

soapbox
1213 Dalon Rd. ste#7 Atlanta Ga 30306

soapbox
1213 Dalon Rd. ste#7 Atlanta Ga 30306 P 4048157557 F 4048157558
John "JC" Richardson

1213 Dalon Rd. ste#7
Atlanta   Ga   30306
P 4048157557
F 4048157558

surprisingly given the company name, everything we created for Soapbox was very clean, medicinal and clinical looking. When they asked us to design a promotional kit for them we decided to continue the theme by creating a detergent box which contained a T-shirt, VHS tape, business cards, stickers, etc. This led to endless research into how to produce an authentic looking box with a perforated pull tab opener and

which used the studio's own coloring. We worked with a copywriter, Rebecca Paoletti, to produce some suitably phrased text and though it was a total pain in the ass to achieve, it was well worth it in the end. We even put little bags of detergent at the top of the box to be the first thing a person saw when they opened it, just to give it a truly authentic feel.

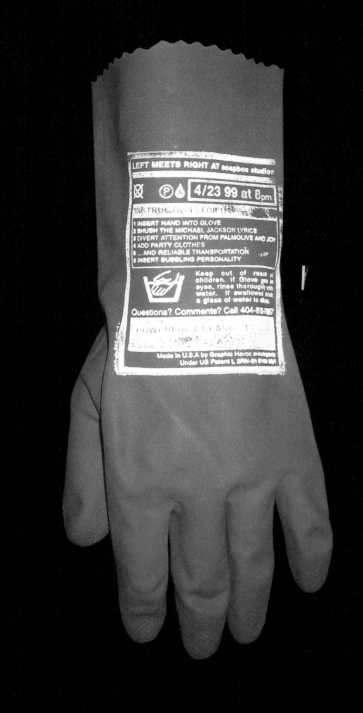

Text on glove label:

LEFT MEETS RIGHT AT soapbox studios

4/23 99 at 8pm

INSTRUCTIONS FOR USE

1 INSERT HAND INTO GLOVE
2 SHUSH THE MICHAEL JACKSON LYRICS
3 DIVERT ATTENTION FROM PALMOLIVE AND JOY
4 ADD PARTY CLOTHES
5 ...AND RELIABLE TRANSPORTATION
6 INSERT BUBBLING PERSONALITY

Keep out of reach of children. If Glove gets in eyes, rinse thoroughly with water. If swallowed drink a glass of water to dilute.

Questions? Comments? Call 404-816-7857

POWERFUL CLEANSING

Made in U.S.A by Graphic Havoc avisualagency
Under US Patent L SPIN-Dh 0198 0698

So, having designed their logo and promo kit, Soapbox asked us to design an invitation to their opening party. This was not long after we had been designing hundreds of flyers and to be honest we were pretty sick of printing on paper. This seemed like an ideal opportunity to experiment with a different kind of material. What could be more appropriate for a

company called Soapbox than a printed rubber glove? We were so excited when we found out that we could get gloves that were exactly the right color, and we spent a long time doing tests to make sure that we could print onto them without the ink cracking or falling off. Then we set up a production line in our studio, blank gloves on one side, printed and

drying g
and more
over the
up on th
insistenc
througho
When th
someone
back a y
name wr

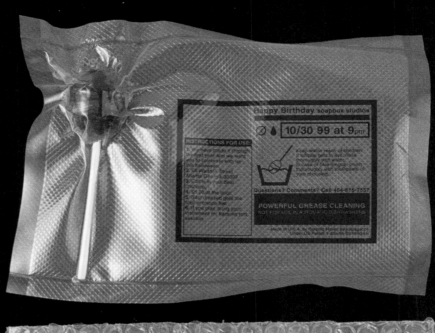

Soapbox's first anniversary coincided with Halloween and we decided to incorporate Blowpops into the party invitation. In keeping with the look and feel of the whole identity, the language was all very clinical and clean while the lollipops themselves were, obviously, blue. We unwrapped them and then vacuum-sealed each one by hand to create envelopes, which were mailed out. We were super enthusiastic about doing all this fresh shit and equally happy to have found a client prepared to let us do whatever we wanted – and pay us for it. Weirdly, this was one of the only clients we lost when we moved from Atlanta to Brooklyn, but that was more a question of circumstances than anything else. We still have total respect for all the people there, and are really proud of the work that we produced for them.

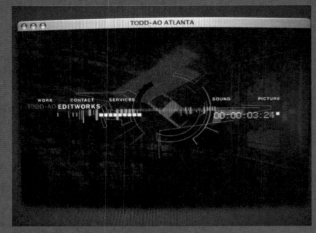

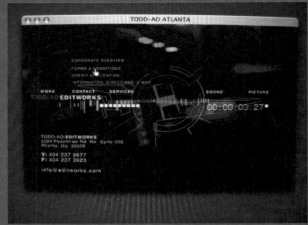

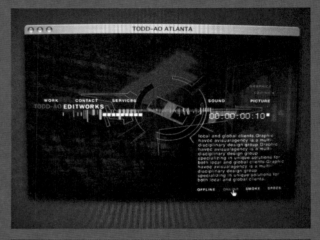

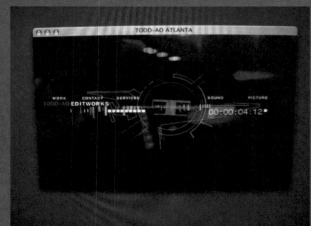

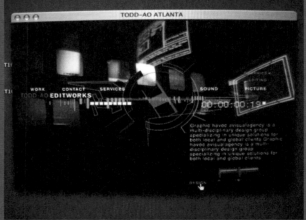

Todd-AO Edit Works
TODD-AO EDIT WORKS
Website (design draft)
1997

We designed this website for an Atlanta post-production house not long after we'd done the Gonz site for adidas. They came to us and said that they wanted a website that looked unlike anything else, something "crazy". So we went to their studio and photographed things we found in their tape rooms (lights, gauges, monitors, lots of blurred abstractions). We used these as background images, which would load in randomly when you first arrived at the site. The navigation system itself was in the center of the screen, with information loading in above and below. Nobody was doing this kind of shit at the time; in fact, you still don't see it much though, of course, it's become more common. Anyway, it didn't really matter in the end because the site never actually went live.

Arnold Communications
RADIOVW.COM
Poster Illustration
2001

RadioVW.com was Volkswagen's digital radio site, and their ad agency asked various designers to come up with an image to "illustrate music". As we're not particularly known for one illustration style (unlike most of the others they commissioned) we tried to answer this almost impossibly open brief as directly as we could. And as VW is a car company, we tried to incorporate a sense of the open road into the image, too. The use of bold color was also extremely deliberate, and just seemed appropriate to what VW was about at the time. The idea was to create something that felt timeless but appropriate, and we must have been at least a little successful, because they continued to use the image for years afterwards.

Elaine Gardner, Shalini Vora
SCOUT
Logo, identity, store environment, promotional materials
1999-2004

Scout was so named because the two founders were sourcing things that Atlanta didn't have. It was like our very own Colette, stocking accessories, men's and women's clothing and stuff that just wasn't available anywhere else. We were (and still are) good friends with both of those lovely ladies and we really wanted to help make sure that their business was a success so we did a hell of a lot of work for them,

including designing their identity and logo, business cards, mailers...

At the very beginning we helped to design the store environment itself, which included a custom-designed cash wrap (a huge, monolithic beast). The shelving was very simple and minimal: massively thick shelves that came directly out of the walls. Finally, we nominated a couple of walls on which we displayed artworks,

switching them out each season to coincide with the themes, colors and textures of the new stock.

In fact, we pretty much changed everything each season in order to fit the prescribed new look. Even the Scout identity itself constantly evolved. One season it was all to do with scenes from the classic Stanley Kubrick film *The Shining*. We featured these super large-scale tile

photographs of Jack Nicholson and Shelley Duvall in the store itself and used that tile look as the basis for all the other materials we produced. Another time Scout held a "monster summer sale", so what else could we do but produce a load of flyers and mailers featuring monster trucks? (As it happens we also designed some truck animations for their website). We probably went a bit overboard, truth be known, we really did oversee everything right down to the shopping bag. But it was a labor of love and to this day Scout is still considered one of the coolest stores in Atlanta (it's always being featured in some mag or other) so it all worked out pretty much exactly according to plan.

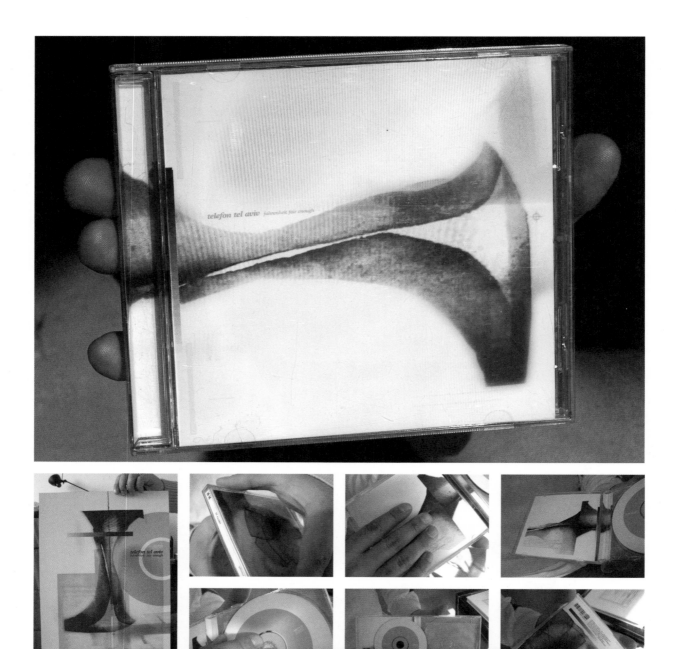

Hefty Records
TELEFON TEL AVIV
Fahrenheit Fair Enough
Album packaging, posters, & promotional materials
2000

This group's music is very digital sounding and we wanted to reflect that in our designs for them. The band were friends with an assistant of the artist Francesco Clemente, and they managed to get the rights to use some of his paintings on the album sleeve. We clipped out a part of one of the paintings to use as the basis for the whole identity system. Having digitally photographed it while it was on the computer monitor, the reflections caused these beautiful scan lines: we thought of the end result as a bit like a digital watercolor. Turns out Clemente himself didn't agree and wasn't that into what we had done, which was a bit of a bummer, to say the least. We did use other pieces of his work inside the booklet and on the back cover, which we left completely untouched, so hopefully he wasn't too horrified by the whole thing.

Graphic Havoc
**THE ELIZABETH
KENT STORY**
Self-promotional book
2000

This was our first ever book, though the unkind might be tempted to call it a pamphlet. We had done the identity system for local Atlanta printers Thomas and Bohannon (more later) and in return they produced the book for us for free. Perhaps unsurprisingly, we used special printing effects and metallic inks throughout while most of the book was printed in four colors – even though at the time Thomas & Bohannon only had a two-color press (some of the pages were even put through three times for a totally gluttonous six color effect). The content was a mix of personal work and pieces we all worked on while the title came from blending the names of the two streets we had worked on at that point: Elizabeth in Atlanta, Kent in Brooklyn. Essentially it was a (really small) coffee table art book, but it sold out immediately and we couldn't have been happier.

Keywords
MULTIPLE "LOGO" ID DEVELOPMENT, 1 COLOR, UNCOATED PAPER

Concurrent Events
DAVID GOES TO THE LAND OF THE RISING SUN, FOR A GIRL

Brad McDonald
BRAINWASH MARKETING
Corporate identity
1998

This was a new company that opened in Atlanta. They were about guerrilla marketing: stickers, flyers, posters, etc. We decided that their identity should be equally in-your-face and hint at the literal meaning of their name. So we enlarged various well-known symbols to hint at the idea of their forcing ideas into your brain. There was nothing subtle about what they were doing and so there was

nothing subtle about our designs. All of the employees in the company got a different image on their business card: one of them was a photograph of a tank that we got off the web and then altered. The type was a fucked up version of Trade Gothic while the whole thing was printed on colored paper in this gunmetal grey color that somehow echoed the grungy, dirty feel of the whole thing.

Coca-Cola
COKE BOTTLE WRAPS
Packaging drafts for Japanese market
2000

We were commissioned to come up with ideas for Coke bottles that were specifically aimed at the Japanese market. So we went down various paths: some of our designs were totally kitsch and cute, others looked completely cyber and techno. Still others were inspired by nature, using imagery of trees and typically Japanese bamboo, while we also invented a family of characters, giving them all individual personalities. The label would explain who the animal was and then list its friends, who would be featured on other labels. The idea was that people would want to reunite all of the friends and would try and collect the set, that whole "bottle as collector's item" idea.

These were actually produced for a marketing meeting in Tokyo and we have no idea if any of them were ever mass produced (though Coke owns all of the designs so could still use them now if they wanted to). Still, we did a lot of work for the presentation so we thought we'd include them here.

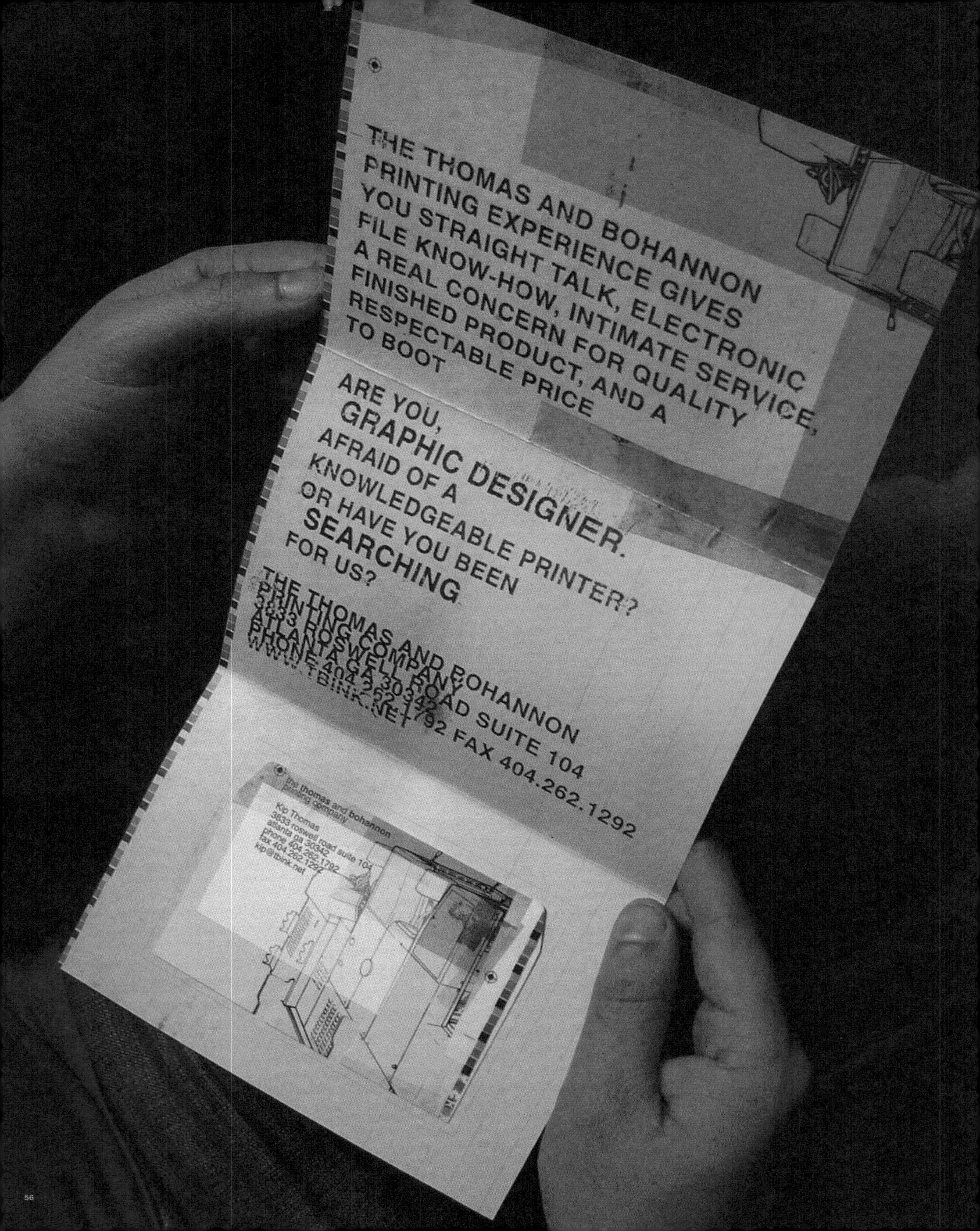

THE THOMAS AND BOHANNON PRINTING EXPERIENCE GIVES YOU STRAIGHT TALK, ELECTRONIC FILE KNOW-HOW, INTIMATE SERVICE, A REAL CONCERN FOR QUALITY FINISHED PRODUCT, AND A RESPECTABLE PRICE TO BOOT

ARE YOU, GRAPHIC DESIGNER, AFRAID OF A KNOWLEDGEABLE PRINTER? OR HAVE YOU BEEN SEARCHING FOR US?

THE THOMAS AND BOHANNON PRINTING COMPANY
3633 ROSWELL ROAD SUITE 104
ATLANTA GA 30342
PHONE 404.262.1792 FAX 404.262.1292
WWW.TBINK.NET

the thomas and bohannon
printing company

Kip Thomas
3633 roswell road suite 104
atlanta ga 30342
phone 404.262.1792
fax 404.262.1292
kip@tbink.net

the thomas and bohannon
printing company
3833 roswell road suite 104
atlanta ga 30342

Kip Thomas and Bruce Bohannon

THE THOMAS & BOHANNON PRINTING COMPANY

Corporate identity, various promotional materials
1999

Sadek actually met Kip and Bruce before the rest of us did: all three of them were into punk music and Kip and Bruce played in a really good local band. They bought a printing company complete with two-color press and quickly became known as *the* printers in Atlanta. After a while, they invested in another press and asked us to design their corporate identity. In return, they printed our first book, *The Elizabeth Kent Story* (see earlier). Kip gave us the manual for the printing press itself and we used

that as our starting point: an image of the press also appears in a lot of the work. Then we focused on the detritus of the printing process, incorporating crop marks, registration marks, CMYK color bars and all the stuff that usually gets cropped off at the end of a job. For the promo mailer, Kip supplied us with the copy which we printed out, cut into strips, glued down onto a piece of paper and then rescanned in order to lay out the final design. We also stuck on a ready-printed Rolodex card.

They printed it as a four-color process job through their two-color press (so each page had to be printed twice) and the end result was fantastic. The only real worry was their studio Siamese cat, who got totally fucked on the fumes, though it certainly wasn't the first – or last – time that happened.

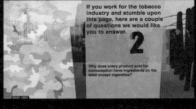

ABCDEFGHIJKLMNOP
QRSTUVWXYZ12345
67890!@#%&*()":?/

...pin Porter and Bogusky: Alex Bunard
EN-SWAT.COM
...osite
...0

SWAT stands for Students Working Against Tobacco. It's a Florida-based organization and is basically the youth-focused arm of the Truth campaign. We were commissioned to design their website and they kept telling us how much they loved our hand-drawn work and wanted something similar. So we created a typeface by hand, taking a printout of the alphabet in either Franklin or

Railroad Gothic (can't remember which now), holding it against the window and then tracing around the letters. We scanned that in and the end result was the font, *Idea's Trace*, which we used throughout the site.

We fixed the navigation system as a column on the left of the screen with a series of links to choose from. This section used an orange camouflage

look (already part of SWAT's existing identity) with very short introductory animations when you finally clicked on what you wanted to read. The site contained an enormous amount of information, and our aim was to make it all as accessible as possible while still being interesting to look at.

CLAIRE
©MCMXCVIX

MILFORD THOMAS
Direction and Scenario

MICHAEL BREWER
Scenic Design

TODD ROBERTS
Costumes

AND

Kathleen Matuszewich
Audrey Pickett
Keribeth Wilson

as the
WATER NYMPH DANCERS

CHOREOGRAPHED BY:
Miriam Arensberg

CLAIRE

Produced, Directed, Written by..........Milford Thomas
Director of Photography..............Jonathan Mellinger
Assistant Camera..........................Pat McDonnell
Production Designer......................Bentley Wood
Set Designer............................Michael Brewer
Musical Composer........................Anne Richardson
Costume Design..........................Todd Roberts
Gaffer....................................Don Cely
Key Grip.................................Dan Philipp

Studio space provided by:
ZONOLITE ROAD PROPERTIES III, LLC.

Titles by:
GRAPHIC HAVOC
avisualagency

Thank You

MR. GEORGE CHANG

For Your Constant Support
of This Film

Milford Thomas
CLAIRE
Film titles
1998

Director Milford Thomas shot this film on 35mm black-and-white film, using an old, hand-cranked movie camera. The final film was one hour long, a silent, Japanese fairy tale with a score written for an orchestra. It took Milford years to complete it while he mostly financed the whole thing himself: it was a real labor of love.

Milford's biggest concern was to make the titles look and feel like the rest of the film: he was adamant that he didn't want something digital or crisp destroying the atmosphere and ruining the beginning and end of the film. At first none of us had any idea what to do, but in the end we put together all the graphics using materials that Milford supplied to us. It was a real cut-and-paste job: even the logo was built out of lots of different elements. When the graphics were finished, we output the digital files onto 35mm slides, which we projected onto a wall. Finally, Milford filmed these projections with his camera in order that the titles have the same lighting, motion, and look/feel as the film itself. It was something of a laborious process but the result was perfect for the film and it was a really special job to work on. This is still the only film title sequence we have done, though of course we'd happily do more.

Keywords
MUSIC PACKAGING, COLLAGE, ILLUSTRATION, PHOTOGRAPHY

Concurrent Events
RANDALL GETS MARRIED, WE ALL EAT BROWNIES

Chocolate Industries
URBAN RENEWAL PROGRAM
Album packaging, posters, & promotional materials
2000

It feels kind of crazy to go straight from the beautifully detailed title sequence we did for *Claire* to this, but it's an undeniably persuasive way of showing off our own eclecticism...

This was a compilation album released on the label, Chocolate Industries. It was a really big release for them but they gave us surprisingly little direction other than that they wanted it to look unlike everything they had released before. At that time Sadek was very into taking

photographs out in the street, of construction work and building apparatus: random piles of stuff you see everywhere (but which most people ignore). We decided that the title of the album and the nature of the music (mainly hip-hop) perfectly lent itself to some of those images. Meanwhile, we had already done a few collage-styled projects so we used the photographs in conjunction with others the rest of us had taken and illustrations that we drew specifically for the project.

We ended up producing ads and a poster as well as the album, 12" and CD covers and the jewel case liner. There was also a 24-page booklet which Chocolate themselves curated, giving a spread each to various "urban" artists like Evan Hecox, Delta, Kaws – and us.

CONSOLIDATED FICTION

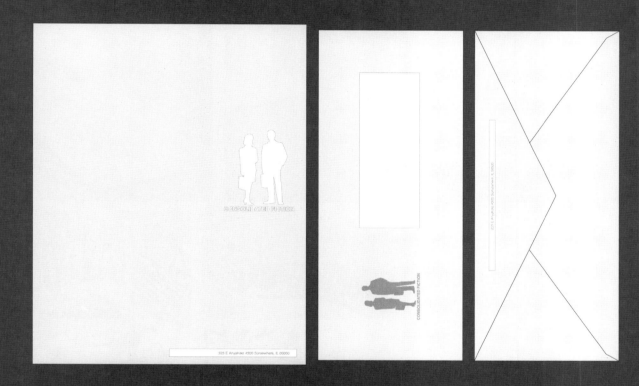

John Hughes II
CONSOLIDATED FICTION
Corporate identity
1999

As you may have noticed, we have designed a lot of sleeves for Hefty Records, which is run by one John Hughes. John's father, John Hughes II, directed pretty much every cult 80s film you can think of (*Pretty in Pink, The Breakfast Club* and *Sixteen Candles,* to name but a few) and we decided that it would be right and proper for us to nag John Jr. to put us in touch with his dad. Rather to our

surprise he did just that and John Sr. called and asked us to work on a logo for his new film production company, Consolidated Fiction. We were very into this idea, and ended up doing around 40 different logo drafts.

The final identity has its origins in a series of artworks that Randall had been working on just before and after we made the move to New York.

These were all loosely based around texts by the likes of the Situationists, Guy Debord and Raoul Vaneigem and we enjoyed the irony of having such revolutionary texts provide the framework for a corporate logo. The icons of the businessman and woman represent both corporate greed and the nameless/faceless nature of the Hollywood executive system (well, to us they do).

arkitip exhibition 0002 new york 21 june 2001
graphichavoc avisualagency
alife

62

Arkitip Magazine/Etnies/alife
EXHIBITION003
Group art show and collateral materials
2002

We hadn't been living in New York that long when Scott Snyder of Arkitip Magazine invited us to take part in a group show that he was curating in a Lower East Side store, alife. The show also featured Green Lady and an old friend from Atlanta, David Kinsey, who collaborated on work to hang inside the store. We were given the two windows up front and the (in our eyes rather random) theme of the show: Future City.

We decided to use the concept of a ship in a bottle and commissioned two huge wooden boxes to be made. We painted and drew on them in the basement of the building our studio was in. It took eight people to lift each box, and they only just fit in the windows at alife: each one was about two inches away from the glass. We also produced artwork to be used on limited edition skateboard wheels as well as posters and stickers. This was

the first show we had taken part in as a collective and it was something of a triumph for us: we had suffered a bit of attitude when we first turned up in New York ("who do these kids think they are?") but by doing this we proved not only that we were extremely serious but also that we were more than competent. To this day, commercial clients still ask us if we can't just reproduce these boxes for them.

The campaign for the previous year's U.S. Open had featured various tennis stars, using the white lines of the court as the basis for the background imagery. The whole thing had a really computerized look and was a really great concept but they asked us if we could push it even further.

We were given all of the photography, which we treated because it was going to be blown up very large (these ads were up huge in Times Square and on busses, trains, phone booths and magazine ads). We cut out the players, re-rendered their outfits and treated their skin tones to make it all look as flat as possible. Then, instead of using the white lines of the court we chose to have these bursts of energy radiating from the players themselves.

The end result was loosely inspired by Japanese war posters: the idea was to make them look totally iconic and impressive, while we also produced a load of other materials to coincide with the whole tournament.

Hefty Records
PHIL RANELIN
Album packaging & posters
2001

Hefty re-released two albums by the legendary jazz musician, Phil Ranelin: *The Time Is Now!* and *Vibes From The Tribe*. They pretty much asked us to use the original sleeves but to update them a bit. Design wise, it wasn't a particularly exciting job for us, but we produced this cool poster on which we used an amazing shot of Ranelin and entirely new design elements, taking our visual cues from the original era. Later on, John [Hughes, of Hefty] commissioned

some musicians to remix original Phil Ranelin tracks. We designed the sleeve for that album, too (right), incorporating photography of original material that John found somewhere, like tape reel boxes, documents, images, that kind of thing. We piled it all on a table and then photographed it, using one of the shots as the main front cover image. We used this rather nutty type on the back, again hinting at the original era but also creating something completely fresh and new.

you are cordially invited to

Graphic Havoc's
THIS PLUS THIS EQUALS THAT
The Elizabeth Kent Story book release opening

scout™
1198 Howell Mill road suite 114
Atlanta, GA 30318
Phone: 404.605.0900
www.scout101.com

Thursday, March 21
7-10pm

live music performance by:
Eastern Developments
special guest dj **Dirty Doctor**
Light fare provided by:
Commune
sponsored by:
Elemental magazine

Graphic Havoc
BOOK LAUNCH PARTY
Invitation, graphics, in-store paintings
2001

To celebrate the launch of our book, *The Elizabeth Kent Story*, we went back and threw a book launch party/art show in Atlanta. When we first moved to New York we discovered this brand of beer called Ballantine. It was dirt cheap and we drank a lot of it. Not that we needed much encouragement but we drank even more when we realized that 22oz bottles included these weird graphics on the inside of the cap which spelled out well-known phrases like 'Pink Panther'. It was a hot idea, which we promptly borrowed to make some murals for our launch party. We made up some new phrases (such as 'Dirty South') and then overlaid all the graphics in this huge installation. We also took some original images from Ballantine ads as the basis for some other paintings and hung up press sheets from the book. Nobody had any idea that the graphics meant anything but it didn't matter, the party rocked all the same.

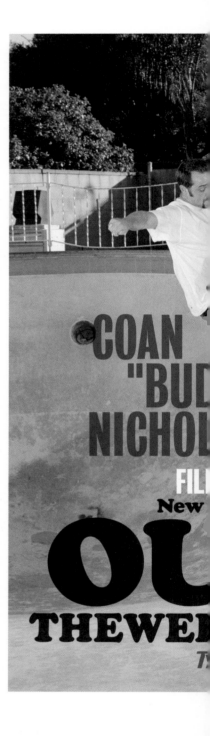

Faith Popcorn's Brain Reserve
TYLENOL: OUCH
Posters, various promotional materials
2003

The Ouch campaign was this huge deal, an attempt by Tylenol to make itself somehow relevant to 18-24 year olds. Una Kim at Faith Popcorn's Brain Reserve, a trend forecasting company, oversaw it while art directors Isaac Ramos and Jerry Lim brought us on board. We worked on various aspects of the campaign, including snipe posters, all of which specifically promoted their website

(ouchthewebsite.com) and a fanzine-style magazine which was distributed along with titles like Tokion and The Fader and featured professional snowboarders, skateboarders, break-dancers, etc... All of the photography was shot and supplied to us by Tobin Yelland.

We also produced two promotional kits for them. The first was for a

conference in New York City called *Creativity Now* and was a kind of "instant creativity" kit: it had marker pens, a sketchbook, blank CDs (and Tylenol) in it. We came up with statements like, "great pain leads to great art (so they say)", spray-painted them onto craft paper and then photographed people holding the signs: the resulting shots were used as the main images. Our client told us

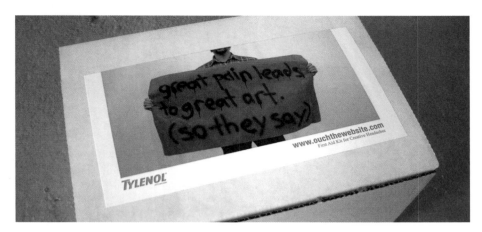

that they were going to be given to all the attendees of the conference but in the end they just went to the speakers. Why Matthew Barney would want a Sharpie marker with 'Ouch' written on it is anyone's guess.

The second kit made a bit more sense to us and was produced to celebrate Tylenol's sponsorship of a skate bowl in Greenpoint, Brooklyn.

There was a big launch party and the next morning they couriered this kit to everyone who'd been there. It contained mints, water (and Tylenol) and there was a sticker on the front saying, "we saw you at the party last night and thought you might need this." It was the perfect hangover kit, except for the fact that for whatever reason they didn't want to call it a hangover kit.

Ben Velez
TRIPLE FIVE SOUL
Ad campaign
Fall, 2002

This was our first ad campaign for a clothing company and we were told that they specifically wanted us to do something completely different from their previous campaign (black and white photography of models on a plain white background). The only rules were that we had to use their existing slogan, "define your soul", and their bags had to feature prominently. So we took that literally and the ads pictured the supposed contents of each particular bag, to show the "soul" of that particular person.

One of the biggest things here was that we didn't get to choose the photographer. They booked B+, who has done some amazing editorial work but had never worked on an ad campaign like this. And it was a bit of a problem. None of the resulting photographs were at all what we had expected and we ended up having to clip the models out of the background altogether. The final ads were much more graphics-intensive than we had anticipated and we weren't really that happy with them (magazine ad shown above). Thankfully, the point-of-purchase work and the look book (left) turned out much better so it wasn't a total disaster.

Hefty Records
SAVATH + SAVALAS
Folk Songs for Trains, Trees and Honey
album sleeve and promotional materials
1998

We were given the photograph to use on this record sleeve; it was a faintly bizarre found image taken at an airport or some similar place. But apart from being supplied with the image, we were allowed to do whatever we liked.

We tried to keep the design really stark and simple. We had always admired those classic, old school albums on the Blue Note label and the idea here was to allow the photograph

to come through as strongly as possible. As such, we enhanced some of the elements of the architecture with a subtle wave illustration. Then we concentrated on ensuring that the type was perfect and beautiful, again dictated by the look and mood of the image and the music.

The other interesting thing was that we were able to use clear plastic inside the Digipak, so we were able to

have a flood of color on the inside. We grant that some people might not find that in any way interesting, but these are the issues that occupy a designer's life.

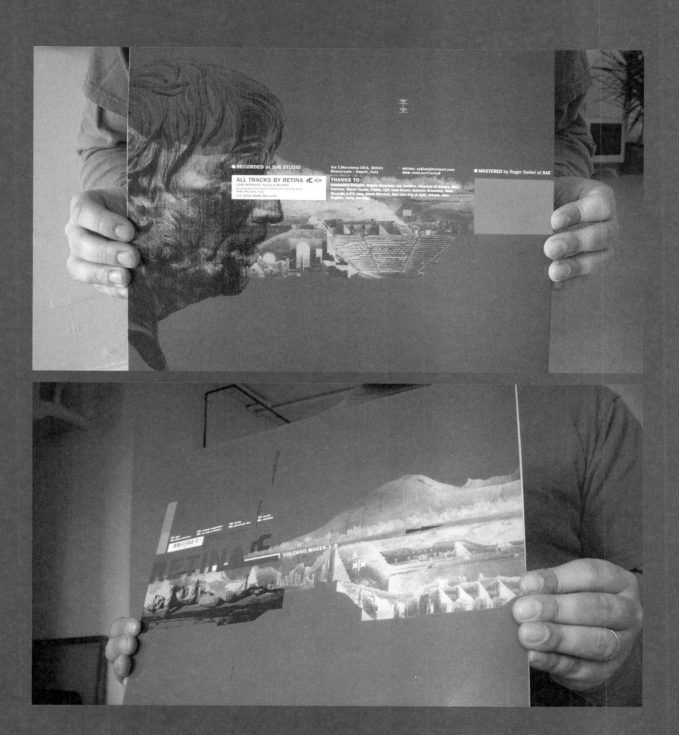

Hefty Records
RETINA
Volcano Waves 1-8
Album design
2001

Retina was a duo of musicians from Italy and they wanted their heritage to be reflected in their sleeve design. The music itself is pretty dark so it made sense to use some imagery from the volcano eruption at Pompeii.

We used some interesting printing techniques on the sleeve and had the text run along the center of both sides. We were playing with the ideas of front and back, making them pretty much interchangeable. In fact, it was even more effective than we had

anticipated: David admitted three years later that he'd always thought the back was the front.

This was yet another sleeve for Hefty, though this was also one of the rare times we collaborated directly with the artist. It's always surprising to us that more musicians don't get involved directly with their own sleeve designs, though of course it's something of a blessing too, because it means we only have one client to deal with.

Then, of course, there's the music itself. We do always try to listen to whatever we're designing for (though sometimes that's simply not possible). The real drawback is when we absolutely hate the music, which of course does happen. When we really dislike whatever we're designing for, we try to concentrate on making something that is at least interesting to look at.

55DSL

ALL GOOD THINGS MUST COME TO AN END

Group art show
2002

This was a total free-for-all. 55DSL in New York's Union Square had started putting on art shows in a new gallery space within their store and asked us to do one of them. Back then there was a real craze for flat, graphic paintings and so we decided to make some really flat, graphic paintings, and then fuck them up. We went over them with pencils, spraypaint, magic markers, sharpies... anything to give a layered effect. We painted on huge wood panels that were installed throughout the store, even on the ceiling. It was a true collaboration between all of us that, naturally, led to a certain amount of good-tempered rivalry. For instance, Randall spent hours painting a perfect silhouette of a deer. As soon as it was dry, David drew googly eyes and buckteeth on it. It was all part of it; we knew that we couldn't be too precious about any of it because as soon as it was done someone else would just go over it. If anything it encouraged us all to be more and more outrageous. (See overleaf for images of us all at work).

The final touch was the over-the-top titles we gave each painting: complete nonsense that amicably mocked the pretensions of the art

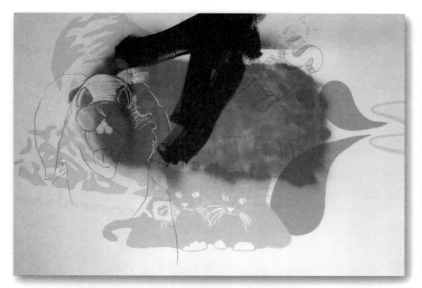

world. One of them was called *Concerns Concerning Uniformity and Deterioration*, while another was *The Inability for the Average Man to Actually Believe Someone Painted This, even*. We subtitled each one *Go For It!*, a phrase which cropped up on some of them. We also made some equally layered T-shirts that were given away at the opening.

Tokion magazine/Nike

NIKE: TIM MONTGOMERY

Magazine ad
2000

We were commissioned by Tokion magazine to design an ad for Nike. The idea was to produce an ad for a specific Nike-sponsored athlete (ours was for sprinter Tim Montgomery) and they asked different artists and designers to produce something based around their existing artistic style. In the beginning it was really exciting and everyone seemed down for doing something genuinely innovative. The idea was to create

an ad reminiscent of old Colorforms kids' toys: there would be a scene with various characters in a situation accompanied by a sheet of stickers so that readers could customize the ad as they saw fit. Sadly, as so often happens when there are lots of people involved (essentially we had clients from both Tokion and Nike), it ended up being a nightmare. The idea of what we were actually producing was changed numerous times and it

turned out that they (Tokion) didn't want to credit the commissioned artists on the ad. In the end we managed to get our name onto the sheet of stickers, but none of the artists who came after us were credited at all. Truthfully, it was pretty aggravating but still, we were psyched to have done an ad for Nike.

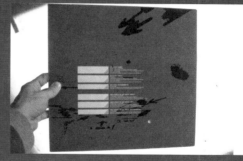

Counterflow Recordings
DAVE GHETTO
Eye Level B/W Wild World of Rap Music &
Love Life, All Time Greats, No Wins
12" sleeve designs
2002

We did a couple of sleeve designs for this hip-hop artist and this is a pretty good example of a job where we didn't hear the music first. But it was hip-hop, so we used references from that world that we thought the musician might be into.

For one of the sleeves we found a photograph of a truck and made an illustration from it, while on the other we used some photography of random street signs and scenes that we pushed together to make the cover image. The type was a fairly simple stencil font, which we left untweaked and used throughout.

Hefty Records
IMMEDIATE ACTION
12" sleeve designs, compilation album sleeve
1999-2000

John Hughes at Hefty came up with this idea of producing his own version of white label 12" records but wanted to have a consistent graphic look for the series, which he called Immediate Action. Of course there's a reason why white labels are white, it's to save time and money, so the sleeves were screen printed as opposed to offset. Then, each time there was a

new release we just had different stickers printed (they can be printed in 48-72 hours). Somehow it all just fit with the concept of doing things on the fly and in the end the series really stood out and it quickly became a bit of a collector's item.

After a while, John decided to produce a compilation album of some

of the releases and we ended up making new stencils to reference each of the records that had been put out up to that point. We went out and sprayed the stencils onto various walls in our neighborhood and then photographed them. It was really refreshing to get back to doing some real, hands-on work. Most of the time you have to spit work out fast and you

can get into a bit of a rut staring at a computer screen all day; this was a nice contrast.

The only truly bizarre thing about the compilation sleeve was that the type was printed in a rather swish gold foil stamp. It was meant to be the yellow of the original series but for no reason at all the printers reinterpreted our instructions and decided to print it with this gold foil. Initially, we were really upset about it but after a while we decided it was so entirely random that we should probably get over ourselves and learn to like it.

TRIPLE FIVE SOUL VS GRAPHIC HAVOC

Art installation
2002

Another art show in a New York City retail space, only this time we took the opportunity to use up every part of the space that was available to us (pretty much all of it, though of course we weren't allowed to fuck with the clothes). We designed these huge prints of completely random imagery all stuck together collage-style. We also made tape installations of an 18-wheeler and a bird, which we stuck onto the front windows of the store. In fact, tape featured a lot throughout the show: we used it (and other materials) to customize a bunch of Triple Five Soul bags, while we ended up having to stick up the prints with tape after we couldn't get them to stay up the way we had wanted.

The theme we decided upon for the show was based on the idea of found objects, so we vacuum packed a load of trash that we found on the street (including a half-eaten sandwich) and stuck it to the wall (with tape). We also put up some of the uncut press sheets from *The Elizabeth Kent Story* and used the opening party as our New York book launch. As you can see from the images, the party was a riot and we all had a fine time.

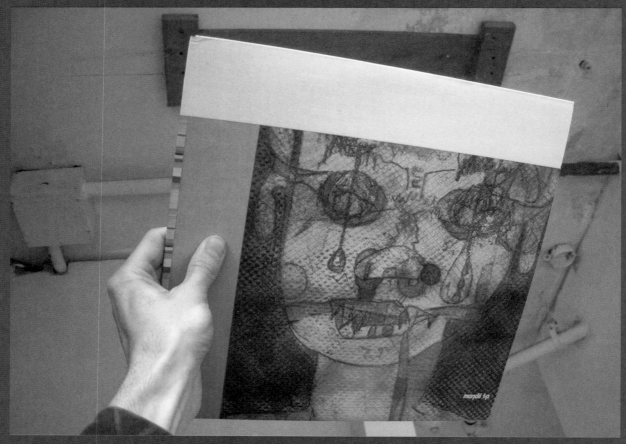

Hefty Records
MONDII
CD and LP design
1999

Mondii is an electronic musician from Japan. He requested that we use these pretty weird, faintly fucked-up looking illustrations that his younger sister had done as the basis for his album cover. That was pretty much the only direction and guidance we were given so as a result we simply allowed the illustrations to dictate our whole design. We designed a suitably bizarre world based on the colors, shapes and mood of her images,

creating our own abstract images for the back cover of the LP.

The CD design was pretty cool, too. This was the first time we were able to print the track listing in the clear part of the inside of the jewel case, with colored bars featured inside the case. Any non-designers out there will just have to trust us that these moments can be genuinely exciting.

Arena Rock Recording Company

ON!AIR!LIBRARY! AND THE ALBUM LEAF

Split EP design
2003

On!Air!Library!'s music is really dreamy. Having been commissioned to design the sleeve of an EP which they put out jointly with another group, The Album Leaf, we seized the chance to use the equally dreamy photography of a talented friend of ours, Bryan Collins.

Bryan donated two images to the project: the front cover image which is a close-up of a flower and the one inside which is an abstract shot of some floral debris. We really wanted to keep everything as clean and simple as possible: it was all about color and the beauty of the images, abstract though they were.

Hefty Records
SCARLET DIVA
LP, CD and promotional materials
2000

John Hughes of Hefty was asked to compose the soundtrack for Asia Argento's directorial debut, *Scarlet Diva* (she also wrote and starred in the film). John wanted us to go down the classic Ennio Morricone route so it made sense for us to hark back to classic film posters from the 1960s.

We were given the photograph to use on the cover; perhaps not surprisingly we decided to show it fairly large. We hand-drew the title of the album while the rest of the typography was based on classic elements from old movie posters and paraphernalia.

We had some other images to use inside the booklet (an insert in the case of the LP) and we messed about with the levels in order to try and make it look like various different colored screen-prints. We used a wine-colored background and various shades of red, deliberately making the background look unregistered in order to achieve a screen-printed look.

People are often surprised to discover that we did this sleeve, but even though it doesn't necessarily scream GH at you, we think it's a classic that will hold up for years to come. Don't get us wrong, we don't think it's particularly ground-breaking design, but we definitely think it's pretty damned good.

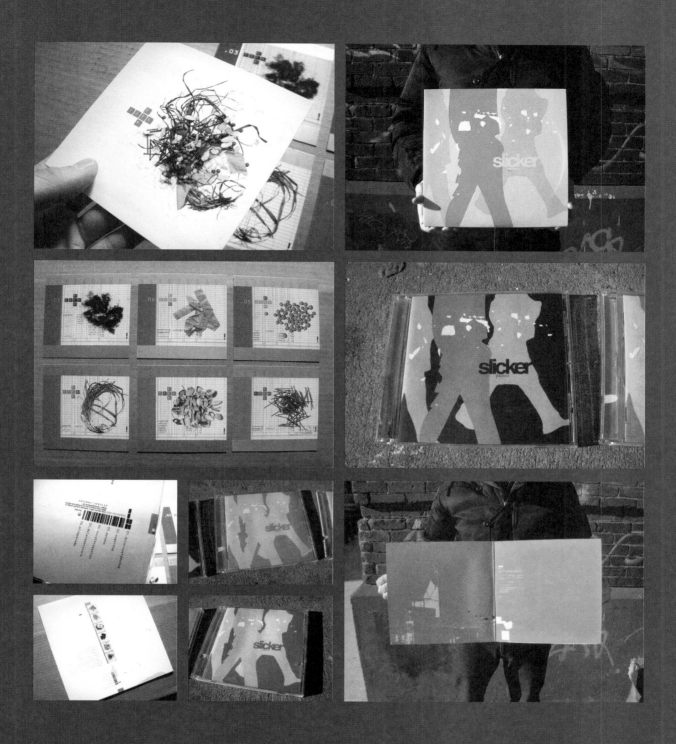

Hefty Records
SLICKER
Album design
1999-2000

More music by John Hughes of Hefty. *Slicker: Remixes* was a remix album of some of his earlier work and there were six tracks on the album. We used random or found objects to represent each one. They were pretty arbitrary objects (including hair and almonds) shot in order to build up an interesting look. The jewel case had six panels as opposed to one booklet and each was reminiscent of those science cards you got at school: an image on one side, the relevant information on the other. The cover itself was a photograph of all of the objects mixed together: remix, see?

A year or so later we worked on *Slicker: The Latest*. John knew he wanted to do something with people walking and he had taken photos of people walking in the streets, but that was about as far as he got. We ended up treating the shots in various different ways and featuring them alongside images of Chicago he'd taken before, mixed up with some of David's photographs. We printed the cover in four different colors so that diehard fans could collect all four (or less diehard fans could buy one in a color they liked). It actually ended up looking a little soft which was really annoying at the time, but then a lot of people told us that they really liked it, so what do we know?

RICHARD DEVINE
Aleamapper LP, CD and posters
2002

More electronic music, this time with a really dark edge to it. We were told that Richard wanted the album sleeve to be based on paintings by the artist Francis Bacon, while we were also given all these graphic images of crime scenes and death to use as the basis for our design.

At first we tried to do something abstract, but it wasn't really working so in the end we went back to basics and created a series of abstract images based on the motion and brush strokes of Bacon's paintings. They were random, abstract, organic shapes that we manipulated, blurred and distorted and then overlaid on this gorgeous dark purple background. Then we overprinted it with this spot UV varnish applied in a really angular way, to try and hint at the corners of rooms that Bacon always seemed to feature. Even if we do say so ourselves, the print job on this was absolutely awesome.

In fact, everything about the album turned out great, apart from one thing: in all the chaos of finishing the job we somehow forgot to credit ourselves. A totally basic error but made even more irritating given how well the final piece turned out. Oh well, live and learn.

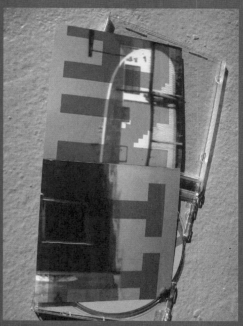

Hefty Records
T. RAUMSCHMIERE
Anti album and Promotional materials
2001

For this particular design we were given a few photographs and the album's title and left to get on with it. Given that the album was called *Anti*, we had plenty to sink our teeth into. We decided that at the very least the sleeve should be anti-design so we put the barcode that usually goes on the back of an album on the front and we blew up the Hefty Records code really large. Then we made an anti-logo for the album title, using letters from various classic corporate logos, such as IBM and Audi.

Truthfully, the photographs that had been given to us weren't that good. That's not meant to sound mean, but in the first place they were digital, of fairly poor quality, and their subject matter really didn't strike us as particularly interesting. To get around this, we decided to crop them, hone in on details that at least caught the eye but also blow them up so large that the end results were totally pixilated. Then we turned them all upside down: the cover image is actually part of a "Dead End" sign.

Finally, we were going to print the brand-based logo we had developed in the CD tray and on the inside of the booklet, but as it turned out that looked pretty bad when enlarged so we ended up using the typeface from the rest of the sleeve, which worked pretty well.

Wieden + Kennedy, New York

X GAMES

Ad campaign, promotional materials
2003

The X Games are an ESPN-produced competition featuring skateboarding, BMX riding, motocross, all types of "extreme" sports. This one took place in summer in Philadelphia (hence the inclusion of the Liberty Bell). They'd already done TV ads, which featured some of the athletes hanging out in front of a convenience store so we took that as our theme. Once that was decided upon we broadened it to include stuff you might buy at a store in the summer, like, well, you know, ice creams and things.

The lettering and the ice cream truck were hand-drawn, while we also came up with various other elements to use in a collage effect throughout the whole campaign. Unnervingly, one draft that included an illustration of a rainbow (magazine spread, bottom right) was nixed for being too closely associated with the Gay Pride movement. We really argued that one but they weren't budging so in the final ads the rainbow was replaced with sunrays. Unbelievable really, but perhaps even more shocking was that

everyone was so casually accepting of this state of affairs. They were totally apologetic and everyone we spoke to said they could understand our point of view but at the same time they were also adamant that we couldn't include it. A rainbow, for fuck's sake! Insane.

Ahem. Moving on, Wieden + Kennedy covered a real ice cream van in a vinyl wrap to make it look exactly like our illustration. We have to admit that was kind of cool.

Various
RANDOM T-SHIRTS
Garment ornamentation
2000-2004

Given that our company was essentially born out of Theft, the clothing line that Randall and Derek started way back, it's perhaps not surprising that we have designed a lot of T-shirts. Over the years we have gone through different phases, often inspired by music and old school skateboarding graphics (David in particular seemed to own every 'Bones Brigade', 'Pushead' and 'Santa Cruz' T-shirt ever made) and we have been regularly experimenting with various materials and placements of graphics.

A lot of companies take an element from an existing piece of design and then just stick it on the front of a T-shirt, but we try to twist it somehow to make it more interesting or at least a little different. Having said that, people will wear pretty much anything these days, so we often end up designing shirts that we might actually wear ourselves. We always seem to use dark colored shirts (because that's what we look good in) and then apply a graphic that we would like to rock.

Kelly Teasley, Maggie White
YOUNGBLOOD GALLERY
Invitations, business cards
1998-2001

These are self-mailer invitations that we designed for an Atlanta-based art gallery. The owners commissioned us to do what we had already been doing for various club nights around town and we took the opportunity to experiment and come up with totally different solutions each time. We would often take just one abstract element of some of the work that was on show, but the bottom line was that we were very definitely trying to avoid making the "here's a piece of work

and where you can see it" style of invitation. Sometimes we'd include ideas from the artist that were relayed to us, but really we were given a huge amount of freedom.

The invitations also gave us the excuse to play around with a lot of type, while we also instituted the YBG shorthand of the gallery's name. And, as much as each one looked very different, there were a number of recurring themes and regular

compositional elements that meant they worked really well as a series, too. Each one was printed in two colors on uncoated paper and they really stood out from everything that was around at the time. In fact, the invitations have become a collector's item, which is always a gratifying endorsement of your work. Randall and Sadek actually ended up exhibiting there as well, they put on a group show together with the photographer, Bryan Collins.

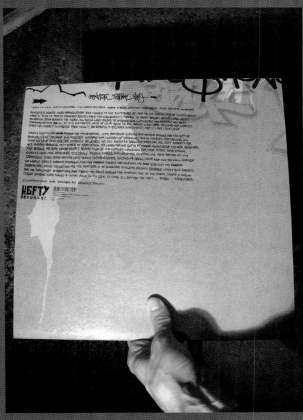

Hefty Records

BENEATH AUTUMN SKY
Album design
2002

Derek actually went to elementary school with Smaze, one of the two musicians behind this release, while he had known the other, Zane III, since junior high. So when it turned out that our first ideas for their album sleeve weren't really working so well, he felt that he should contribute something more similar to his personal artwork.

We are all pretty strict about the lines between commercial and personal; it's really important for us to maintain a tension and a balance between them. But due to Derek's close personal history with these two musicians we felt that we could go in that direction and that maybe it would be okay to blur the boundaries for this project.

As such, the whole album sleeve is hand-drawn: only the Hefty logo and the barcode are computer generated. It's a hip-hop album while both of the musicians are also graffiti writers, so that style was definitely appropriate, too. A huge amount of different illustrations were produced, which we then scanned and rearranged in order to create the cover.

Tokion, Complex, Lumpen, Select, Translucent, XLR8R

RANDOM ILLUSTRATIONS
Various magazine illustrations
1998-2004

We did a guest illustration for Select magazine in Chicago that probably changed our lives. Yes, that sounds a little dramatic but it's pretty much true. And what's so funny is that it all actually happened more out of desperation than anything else. We knew that we had to do this illustration but we were all hugely in denial, each one of us secretly hoping that someone else would take care of it. Finally we knew we couldn't ignore the deadline any longer so we decided to force everyone to take

part and contribute elements so we could create the image tag-team style. And the look stuck. For months afterwards we would get calls from people wanting us to reproduce the "Graphic Havoc" style. Initially we were like "eh? What style?"; then we exploited it, and then finally it got a bit boring. But that whole hyper-collage thing was definitely a trend that stuck around for a while.

Around this time we started a section on our website called GH: Other Shit (GHOS). We posted up illustrations and stuff we did in art shows as well as links to our personal websites. Then, before we knew it, we found we were getting a lot of work as a direct result of that. In fact it probably got us more work than our "official" portfolio ever did. Weird.

Keywords
ROCK MARKETING, ILLUSTRATION, CREATIVE CONSULTING

Concurrent Events
DEREK HAS ART SHOW IN TOKYO, DAVID JUMPS OUT OF A PLANE AND LANDS ON A BAR STOOL

Psyop
FUSE
Promotional booklet
2003

This is by far and away the ugliest thing we have ever produced, but it was meant to be damned ugly so we're really proud of it. In fact, making something grotesque can be good fun: designers seem to get so obsessed with making things look perfect that the obvious next step is to revel in making something where the only thing that is remotely pleasing is that it's all completely displeasing. (Or is that just us?)

Anyway, we were commissioned by the production company Psyop to create the print element of a campaign they were working on for a TV channel. Fuse tries to market itself as MTV's edgier, punk upstart rival, so they wanted the look to be totally messed up. We compiled a series of random images to go along with the text that was supplied to us, though in the end we actually had to edit out a lot of our ideas, which turned out to

be a bit too messed up and edgy. In fact, they needed the finished product ungodly quick so the binding and printing were fairly terrible. But in the end we felt that added to the retarded and revolting nature of the project as a whole.

Kemado Records

KEMADO RECORDS & ELEFANT

Corporate identity, stationery, album, promotional materials
2002

Kemado is Spanish for something to do with fire so we designed their logo comprising red-hot flames. Then we made the rest of their collateral using that well-known (to designers, at least) "80s design trick", which involves taking an element of the logo, blowing it up and then cropping and using just a part of the image. Now we may not be "trained", but to us that pretty much sums up the discipline of graphic design. So, having designed their corporate identity, Kemado asked us to design

their first EP sleeve, for a band called Elefant. We ended up doing a Digipak EP, a poster and a mailer, among other things. Our only real direction as to the look and feel was that they wanted some kind of DIY esthetic: it was at the time when that kind of thing was on the up and up.

Now we have to admit we weren't so into the band's music (it's kind of pop rock) but we took some photographs of street scenery on the West Side of New York and then hand-drew the

typography. We also scanned in some scribbles which we made red and laid over the black and white photography, which is actually an amalgam of a street sign and some clouds.

TRIPLE FIVE SOUL
Ad campaign
Spring, 2003

This was our first shoot with Jody Fausett as photographer, and we went on to work with him on a few subsequent campaigns, too. At this point, the advertising was still based around celebrities, even though we were strongly advocating using models (more professional and at least a bit unlike the other streetwear brands out there...). On this campaign we worked with the likes of Mia Doi Todd, King Britt and Blackalicious, and some of the ads came out great. After the chaos of our first campaign,

we were much more in control of the situation and we built all of the sets ourselves – one for each model.

We gave our models a questionnaire to fill out asking them to "define their soul" (the slogan of the campaign) and then we built a suitable environment for each one. Mia Todd is really into nature and Tibetan artwork so we built a living room with a tree growing out of the carpet, a white tiger carved into the tree and some painted Tibetan skulls.

Everything was built at the back of the Triple Five Soul warehouse because of the budget constraints, but in the main it went down really well and the celebrities were actually quite into the sets we built for them. Actually that's not entirely true – we do have some truly hilarious stories of un-cooperation at its finest – but we'll never tell.

MIA DOI TODD Singer / Songwriter
DEFINE YOUR SOUL triplesoul.com New York City / Fukuoka / Shibuya
For more info on Mia's album "The Golden State" check miadoitodd.com

triple five

EL P Rapper, Producer, Definitive Jux Founder / Owner
DEFINE YOUR SOUL triplesoul.com New York City / Fukuoka / Shibuya
El P's debut solo album Fantastic Damage available now!

triple five

KING BRITT Music Producer, DJ, CEO of Fivesixmedia, Father
DEFINE YOUR SOUL triplesoul.com New York City / Fukuoka / Shibuya
Adventures in Lo-fi, King Britt's addition to the Beat Generation series, available Spring 2003.

triple five

BLACKALICIOUS Gift of Gab (MC / Songwriter) and Chief Xcel (Producer / DJ)
DEFINE YOUR SOUL TripleSoul.com New York City / Fukuoka / Shibuya
www.blackalicious.com

triple five

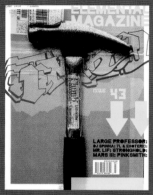

Matt Wright
ELEMENTAL MAGAZINE
art direction and design
2002-2003

Elemental is a Brooklyn-based hip-hop music magazine. We were asked to re-brand and art direct it when their circulation jumped to 75,000.

One of our first ideas was to ask different artists to create an illustration of the word Elemental to be used as the masthead for each issue. When it became obvious that this was going to provide a problem as the magazine's distributor required masthead consistency, we decided to design the headline type 'Elemental' in a font based on Helvetica. We named it Helemental and it was used throughout the magazine. To appease the distributor we devised a scheme to introduce a consistent secondary visual element that would act as an official masthead but basically fall to the background of the title illustrations we received from the artists. The next problem with this concept was that the magazine had no budget for illustrations, so we made it appealing to the artists by suggesting that each artist was given a spread in the publication to do whatever they wanted. Our aim was to create a dynamic and interesting way for the covers to shine on the newsstands.

The response to this was amazing and some incredible artists contributed masthead illustrations such as Jest, Dalek, Crash, Smith, Jaz, Seen, Squirm, Rem, Zephyr, Cycle, and Cap.

Matt Wright
ELEMENTAL MAGAZINE CONTD.
Magazine art direction and design
2002-2003

When we first looked at the magazine in order to re-design it, we were pretty shocked by the crappy quality of the advertising – and by how much of it there was. So our first goal was to try and get some kind of visual flow and pace to the pages. The editorial stories in the magazine are pretty long (most weigh in at around 2000 words), but the whole thing had been a bit cluttered and needed to be stripped back to its bare essentials. Starting at the beginning, we decided

that the contents page should be a full-bleed photograph. It didn't have to be anything specific from the magazine itself, just a good-looking image that somehow encapsulated the essence of that issue. In fact, dealing with the photography supplied, especially in the early days, was also something of a challenge. Writers often seemed to photograph their subjects as well, which meant that a lot of the images were, not to put too fine a point on it, crap. That

didn't really sit so well with our desire to have lots of white space and big, impressive photos so for a while we went the Raygun route and cropped in on details or covered up the image with type. That changed with time as the magazine's reputation grew and photographers began to want to contribute. It was a lot of fun to create a style which wasn't too regimented or strict; we're still proud of this work.

IF I KEEP COMING ATSOMEBODY THESAME WAY IN THESAME FASH-IONTHAT'S NOT TAME LIKE.

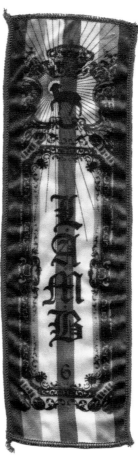

Gwen Stefani and Andrea Leiberman
L.A.M.B
Graphic identity, label, T-shirt graphics
2004

No Doubt front woman Gwen Stefani started up a clothing label called L.A.M.B. the look of which is like Bad Brains opening for The Basement 5 and Linton Kwesi Johnson at the Vatican, with Vivienne Westwood designing the flyer. It's punky reggae with a Catholic overtone: we even suggested making the hangtags like the woolen scapulars given away at first confessions in the Catholic church. The working environment was extremely collaborative which is rare in big projects where often the clients are afraid to cede any control. But Gwen and Annie Younger, her lead apparel designer, knew exactly what they wanted, making the whole process focused, efficient and, frankly, ideal.

Various clients
SCREEN DESIGN
2002-2004

Three projects here. Left shows a site commissioned by online magazine The Blow Up for an article discussing issues raised by a Phaidon book, *The Impossible Image*. The book featured some truly amazing photography by the likes of Nick Knight, Norbert Schoerner and Inez van Lamsweerde, all of whom use technology to create images that simply weren't imaginable in previous years. As such, we wanted to leave the images to speak for themselves and for the interface to

remain out of the way, while also nodding towards the Photoshop application interface esthetic.

Next is the site for an old friend and long-time collaborator, Guillermo Scott Herren, aka Prefuse73. Scott's music is very digital, but just as Nick Knight et al aren't blinded or distracted by the possibilities afforded by technology, Scott blends it with many other sources to create a totally unique result. We wanted to mimic

his mix of digital and analog, so we drew directly into the computer and didn't allow ourselves to erase anything. We also commissioned a back-end system so Scott can update it himself. All too often a site looks amazing but is out of date within about ten minutes. On the right are stills from a projection we created for Scott's tour of Japan, which Panasonic later used to demonstrate the movie capabilities of a new cell phone.

Cartoon Network: Sean Akins

TOONAMI: AND 1
Broadcast design
2004

This interstitial was about And 1, a team of sponsored street ball players. Their look was already very graffiti-inspired so when Toonami commissioned us to come up with some title treatments, it wasn't much of a stretch to carry on in that vein.

When graffiti is written on glass, it has these really beautiful translucent layers to it, and that was what we were trying to mimic with this work.

We also referenced the scratches that writers often etch into glass. All of the tags and text were hand-drawn and then animated so that it looked as if they were being drawn straight onto the screen.

Funnily enough, we are pretty wary of taking on graffiti-styled commercial projects. Yes, it's our heritage but early on we realized that for our company to last longer than a year

(or so) we had to avoid being pigeonholed as doing trendy (at that moment) "urban" work.

We all find it fairly amazing that graffiti has become so mainstream (it is, after all, still illegal) and is still so popular. It's also a little depressing that so much of what's used commercially is inauthentic crap. That's not sour grapes, honest. It's just the truth (as we see it).

Ben Velez

TRIPLE FIVE SOUL

Advertising campaign
Fall 2003

Still dealing with the tagline 'Define your Soul', we decided to push our idea of creating fantasy worlds for the various stars of the campaign. Only this time, rather than creating wildly elaborate sets, we got Jody Fausett to photograph them against minimal background sets and then we treated them in post to create an appropriate environment for each one.

The campaign was nearly a complete disaster after we foolishly showed some of the initial shots before

actually doing any of the Photoshop work. Troy, the owner of Triple Five Soul, saw some of them while he was in China, without realizing that the images weren't in any way finished. We got word that he absolutely hated them and had to do a rushed comp of what the campaign was actually going to look like in order to prevent him getting on a plane and coming back to fire our asses.

Thankfully he loved the final campaign and he was brave enough to go with

some of the more unexpected images (Jean Grae's face isn't actually showing in one of the shots). We got a lot of compliments from magazines running the advertising, and from the people taking part, too.

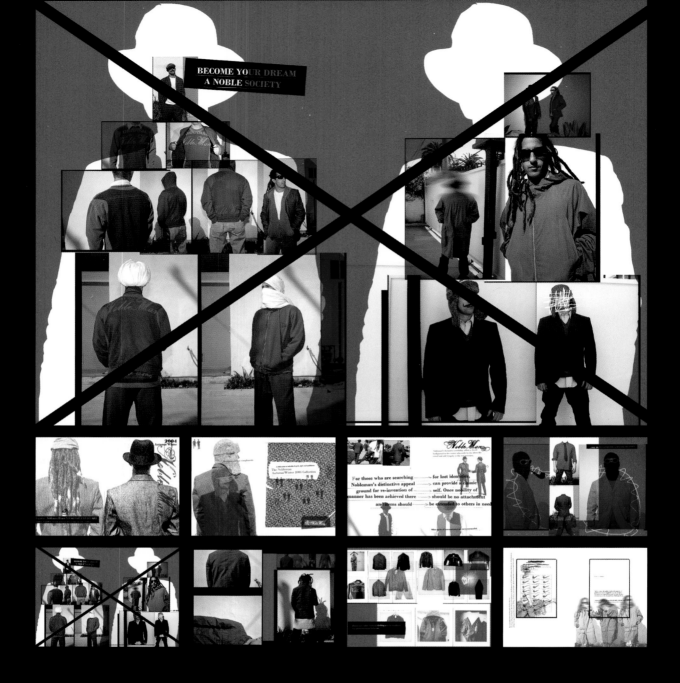

Myles Grimsdale
NOBLEMAN
Look-book
2004

Myles Grimsdale is a super smart, extremely talented, expat Brit who lives and works in Los Angeles, designing for his menswear collection: NOBLEMAN. Myles had got tired of the gaudy graphics and logos that seem to be everywhere in streetwear (with no sign of going away any time soon) and in stark contrast designed a collection of clothes that have a real tailored base to them but are imbued with a spirit of punk rock, hip-hop and traditional elements from early 20th century work clothes. It's both classic and a little bit fucked up!

When he asked us to help him design a look-book to try and explain to potential customers what NOBLE-MAN was all about, we decided that a little bit twisted was the only way to go. We created a 16-page look-book, saddle folded and printed in two colors on really thin paper stock. It was all very

DIY with Peter taking the photographs and the models having their faces cropped or covered so that the details of the clothes stood out.

We used Bodoni as the typeface but printed and cut it out to give it more of an edge. It was rough but functional, satisfyingly like the clothes themselves. of an edge. It was rough but functional, satisfyingly like the clothes themselves.

Savath&Savalas
Apropa't

Warp Records
SAVATH + SAVALAS
Apropa't Album and promotional materials
2004

Having commissioned Maya Hayuk to take photographs of Prefuse73's alter ego Savath & Savalas, we decided against using the images full bleed because it started to look like some awful "chill out" record.

Guillermo Scott Herren had moved to Spain and one of our main concerns was to reflect his new surroundings while also alluding to the previous LP

packaging. The title of the album means "stay close" in Catalan and so we zoomed in on the imagery, made a collage effect with shapes referencing Spanish architecture and laced the whole with a good mix of sans serif headers and serif type body copy.

Scott was keen for the final effect to have the feel of the 1960s or 70s.

We couldn't find the right offwhite paper stock so instead we overprinted with a fifth color tone to make it look right.

Eastern Developments Music
MUSIC PACKAGING
Various Album and promotional materials
2001-2004

Eastern Developments is Peter's side project. It's a fairly informal operation he started with two partners in 2000. They don't really sign artists as such but instead put out records they're interested in. As it's all done extra-curricularly, after the partners' various day jobs, there isn't much time to get hung up on having one strict look for the label as a whole.

In fact, above and beyond the constant use of the logo (actually just the words East Dev) and the legal text, there isn't really one esthetic to the releases. If the musicians are into it then they can get involved, and as long as their ideas work then that's pretty much what will happen. But a lot is thrown together at the last minute, using a lot of hand-drawn imagery (including the promotional posters). Many people help out and the results are super eclectic and strangely satisfying. The idea is to have fun and not take it too seriously.

Warp Records

PREFUSE73: ONE WORD EXTINGUISHER

LP, CD, promos, posters, stickers, ads, invites
2003

For this sleeve we were asked to design "something involving girls" and not to worry about creating a sleeve that looked anything like our previous work for Prefuse73. We decided to take that brief literally (for once) and created something that looked ultra pretty and girly, involving pinks and pastels, which also just happened to feature images of beautiful women. We used photographs of two girls we knew (one of the main images is of Sadek's then girlfriend, Claudia) and we mixed those up with images of other girls we found on, um, various online porn sites.

Obviously we photocopied, distorted and generally messed with the photos of the girls that we didn't know personally so that there wouldn't be any legal ramifications from using images that weren't ours. But really the best thing about this project was that it didn't look like anything you would expect from a cut n' paste electronic hip hop album. The general approach was to create something that felt screen-printed and painterly, something with a hand-made feel that was beautiful and eye-catching.

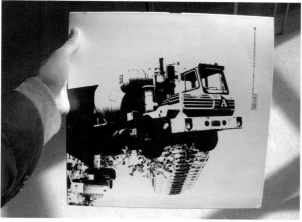

Warp Records
PREFUSE73: ESTROCARO
EP sleeve
2000

This was the first thing we ever designed for Warp Records; the title of the EP is actually in honor of Peter, whose graff name is Estro, and his girlfriend, Carolina (Caro). Scott [Herren] knew that he wanted really hard, grimy and stark imagery to go alongside the music, which is filled with glitches and pops and is quite hard. But at the same time there's quite an organic feel to the music, so the challenge was to combine those elements in the design. In the end we used some photography supplied by Jennifer Smith along with shots we took of cement trucks parked opposite our studio. There's also a faintly random image of Derek's mouth which just seemed appropriate for no particular reason. The large area of white on the cover was meant to have a UV coat on it to create something that was really dirty and gritty underneath but with a clean, inorganic digital block on top. The unfolded sleeve can also be used as a poster: we incorporated all the scoring marks and registration into the design itself.

PREFUSE73: ESTROCARO° WAP134

IN AFRICA, 27 OF 36 ARMED CONFLICTS INCLUDED CHILD SOLDIERS UNDER AGE 15

www.theprop.com

The {PROP}
Peoples Republic of Peace
—— TM MMIII ——

The
{PROP}
Peoples Republic of Peace
—— TM MMIII ——

Mahdis Keshavarz
THE PROP
Corporate identity
2003

The PROP means "The People's Republic of Peace" and was a New York-based organization started up before the beginning of the second war in Iraq. They asked us to work on their corporate identity and after sitting through some brainstorming sessions we decided that the most important thing about them was what they had to say. They really knew what was going on and we thought that was a lot more interesting and relevant than trying to design an eye-catching mark for them.

So what you see here is the logo that we ended up with and our proposal for their letterhead. The idea was that they would print their logo onto plain white paper and overprint a timely statement in one color as often as necessary. That way they could ensure what they were saying wasn't out of date and guarantee a powerful impact. By including their website address we were challenging people to be horrified by what they just read and go and do some research.

We also proposed ambient marketing strategies, such as parachuting foam bombs on New York. Perhaps not surprisingly, given the tense atmosphere here, that didn't ever happen, though ironically it was because of potential fines for littering rather than because it wasn't actually a very good idea.

Cartoon Network: Sean Akins

TOONAMI: AMERICAN WOMEN'S NATIONAL GYMNASTICS TEAM

Broadcast design
2004

This video piece was done for the American Women's National Gymnastics team and featured them talking about their hopes and dreams for the Olympics. All the 16mm footage had already been shot and edited and we were commissioned to come up with graphics to package the piece attractively. We decided to take the ribbons used in freestyle floor gymnastics as our starting point: our graphic versions grew onto the screen, spelled out each individual girl's name and then swooped off screen again. We only had a second per name so it had to be super fast which was something of a challenge but they look really good considering the amount of air time they get.

Yahoo.com
HOTJOBS.COM
Broadcast spot
2003

We were commissioned to do a fully animated TV spot for online job search agency, hotjobs.com, but whereas earlier in our lives Randall had rashly promised the impossible and we'd been forced to admit that we weren't able to produce a fully animated music video, this time we were able to pull it off. In fact, we rocked this job! It took three weeks from start to finish, the client was into it, we were into it... it was perfect.

The idea behind the ad was that the driver was lost, with no direction in life and an urgent need to get back on track (which could be fulfilled by visiting hotjobs.com.). The script called for lots of maps and road icons, most of which we based on our own photography, taken around the world in cities including Tokyo and New York. Having said that, the first map you see is actually of the area around our studio in Williamsburg in

Brooklyn; we found that one online. We did all the animation using Aftereffects as the script required a mix of 2D and 3D effects. Really the only strict rule we had to follow was the defined color palette in order to fit in with our client's existing look and feel. It was all pretty monochromatic looking but it really was an amazingly hassle-free job to work on.

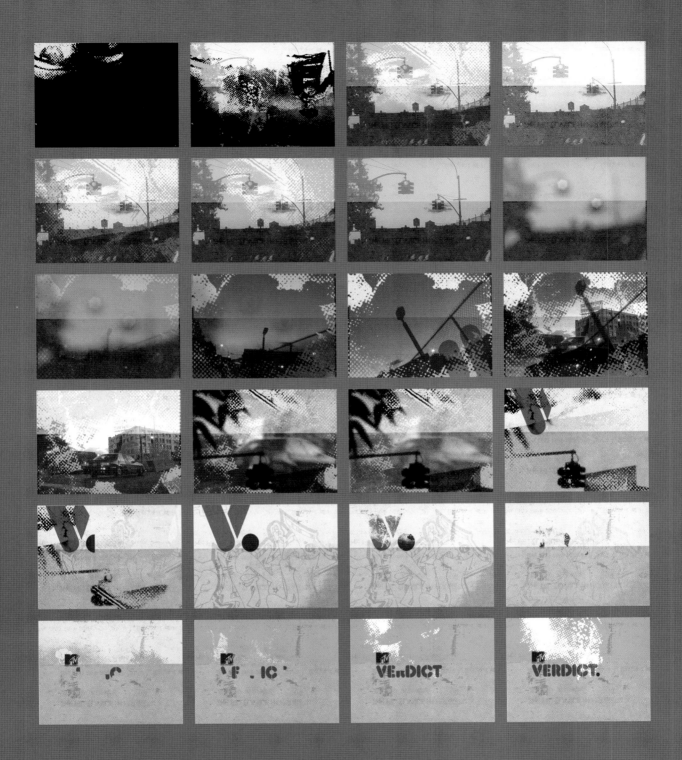

MTV
VERDICT
Broadcast design
2002

Verdict was MTV's answer to that slew of court shows that suddenly appeared on television. It was a pilot for which we developed the identity as well as all of the show's packaging. We got our friend Michael Steed to go out and shoot some video of life in the neighborhood and then used some of the footage mixed with street elements and multiple textures. It was all very MTV, very "uugghh", urban and stylish and not really anything to do with a court at all. We also commissioned the music for the intro, from 431 Music in Atlanta, but we must admit that we have no idea if the show ever aired or not.

Jordan Crane / 55DSL
1 + 1 = 1
Art show
2004

We had admired Jordan's work for a while and then he suggested that we collaborate on something together. He found all these screen prints that he'd done in his undergrad years and offered them to us to do what we wanted with them. The idea was that we'd then put the results up in an art show somewhere. Well, we procrastinated and delayed and did everything we could not to have to work on them and then we could

avoid it no more. So we stayed up very late a few nights, drank a lot of beer and went for it. We were utterly irreverent and the results are entirely random but Jordan assured us that he didn't care what we did and once we got over our reluctance to destroy someone else's work we were away.

Jordan persuaded 55DSL in Union Square in NYC to provide the venue for the show and so we installed

about 50 pieces there. Just before we'd put them up we all stood back and realized that something was missing. Jordan went to a quotation website and found the most surreal comment from the most unexpected source. Yes, Andre Agassi really said: "What makes something special is not just what you have to gain, but what you feel there is to lose". Somehow it fit right in with our own sense of humor and the absurd.

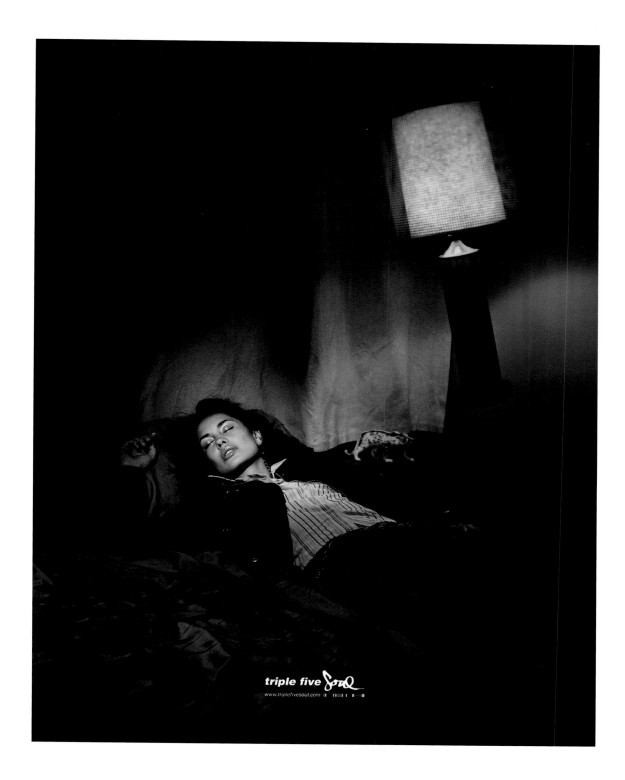

triple five *Soul*
www.triplefivesoul.com

Ben Velez
TRIPLE FIVE SOUL
Advertising campaign
Fall 2004

The concept behind our Fall 2004 campaign for Triple Five Soul was all about abstract communication between people and "the other" via non-traditional devices, showing that the Triple Five Soul audience communicate on a different wavelength to everyone else. We wanted to build on the fantasy feel we had introduced previously in the Fall '03 campaign, while changing the mood to a darker and more mysterious one. We had been admiring the cinematic imagery of LA-based photographer Patrick Hoelck, and felt he would be able to capture what we all saw in our heads, so we commissioned him to shoot the campaign. Working with Patrick, we finished the images by adding subtle lighting effects in post. Once again, we were given a lot of creative freedom by Triple Five Soul which has allowed us to experiment. and try to create work that doesn't look like run of the mill fashion advertising. Later we also took some of the icons from the photo shoot (of antlers and crystals) and incorporated them into other Fall 2004 pieces including the lookbook and a T-shirt graphic.

Jae Shin & Corey Sandelius
ENML
Corporate identity, clothing graphics
2004

These guys first contacted Peter in our LA office to ask him to work on a corporate identity for their company, Deconstruct. Pretty much nothing about the job appealed: there wasn't that much money involved while the name seemed like a relic from the early 90s. Peter blew them off for a bit but then said that we couldn't work for them unless they changed their name. Perhaps surprisingly, rather than telling us to go fuck ourselves, they agreed to do just that – and commissioned us to do the

naming work for them. Initially the company was a crossover streetwear line (later it changed to try to appeal to a more fashion-conscious market) and eventually we decided upon the name Enamel: strong enough to stand out but abstract enough to be long lasting. It's also extremely versatile – if they ever produce a women's line, they've got the whole nail polish idea there just ready and waiting.

We decided not to spell out the name in the logo, so that they could truly

own their identity. We did a lot of logo development (shown here) and we really wanted to stick close to utilitarian principles. However, they wanted to have some kind of icon too, so then our task was to persuade them to go for something simple and versatile. Whenever we develop a marque we try to create something that's classic, simple and not overstated. It can be hard to persuade a client to go for something that seems so simple but in this case they went for it.

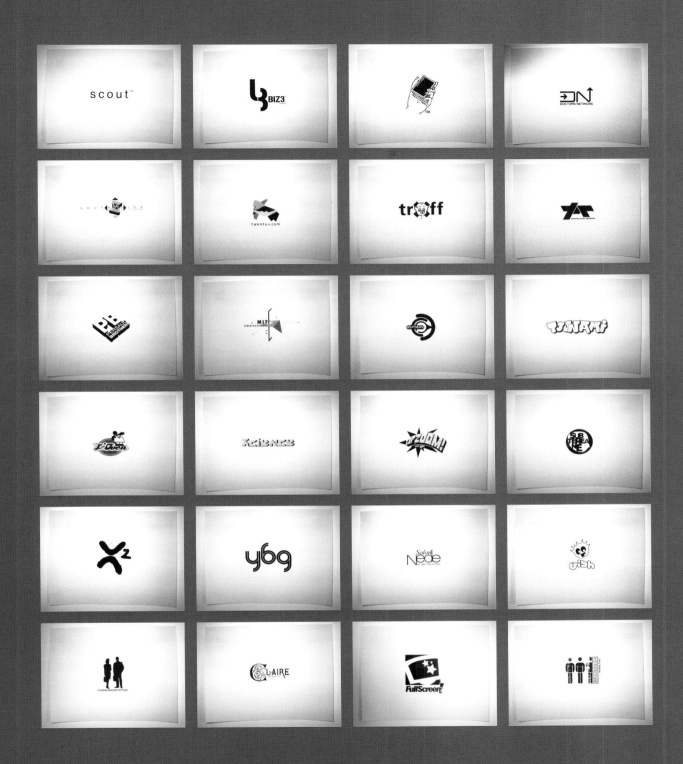

Various
LOGOS
1994-2004

Over the past ten years we have come to realize that some of our favorite jobs are designing logos, corporate identities and working on brand development. In order to make sure that we don't waste our clients' time (or our own) working on something inappropriate, we get them to write down key words about their company: what inspires them, what they're trying to achieve, what they think of when they think about their company, all that kind of stuff. We tell them to be as specific or abstract as they want, and then we take away that list, mull it over and do anywhere from five to 50 designs. One of the really fantastic things about working in a five person collective is that even if one of us is totally lost or stuck for a good idea, chances are someone else will come up with a few good ideas and directions. This page shows some of our favorites so far.

Man vs. Cell Phone

GHavisualagency™

Location
A: Bear Mtn. NY / B: Times Square NYC

Result A
Man   00:05:87
Cell phone   00:29:02

Result B
Man   00:48:08
Cell phone   00:28:60

Experiment
Determine which method of communication is faster across the distance of approximately fifty feet in both urban and rural locations.

Description
On both occasions, the subjects were timed in the successful delivery of a random statement. In one instance, the statement was yelled across the distance. In the other, the statement was delivered via cell phone. Cell phone reception, surrounding noise level, and general location were the main variables in the determination of the final results.

Man vs. Car

GHavisualagency™
special thanks to Camden Turner

Location
A: Bear Mtn. NY / B: 8th Ave & 39th St. NYC

Result A
Man   00:13:54
Car   00:08:15

Result B
Man   00:33:26
Car   01:02:39

Experiment
Determine which method of transportation is faster across the distance of approximately one city block in both urban and rural locations.

Description
On both occasions, the subjects were timed in a race from point A to point B with location being the biggest factor in determinig the end results. Shoes were prohibited as they constitute technology.

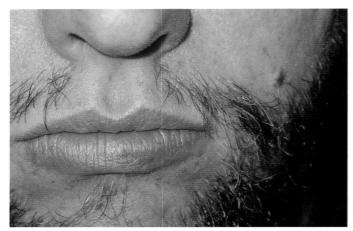 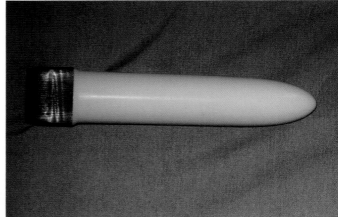

Man vs. Vibrator

GHavisualagency™

Result

Man	13:04:31 (07:00:00 Foreplay)
	(06:04:31 Oral Sex)
Vibrator	01:05:00 (Highest Setting)

Experiment

Determine the faster method to orgasm.

Description

In one instance a woman was left alone with a vibrator and timed on how long it took to achieve an orgasm. The second instance measured how long it took to climax with good old fashioned foreplay and oral sex.

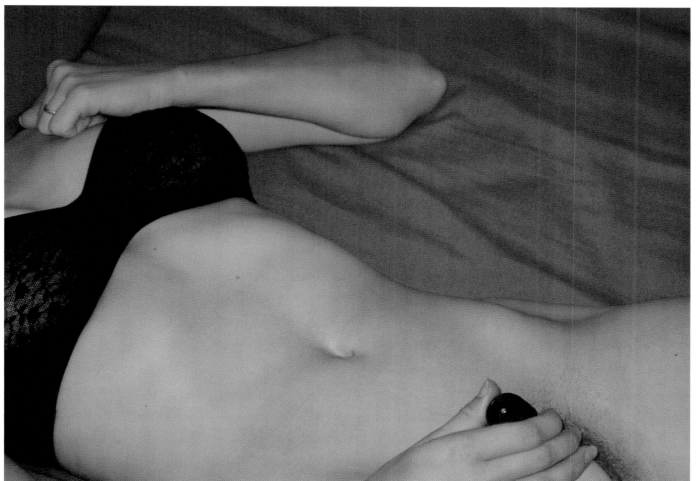

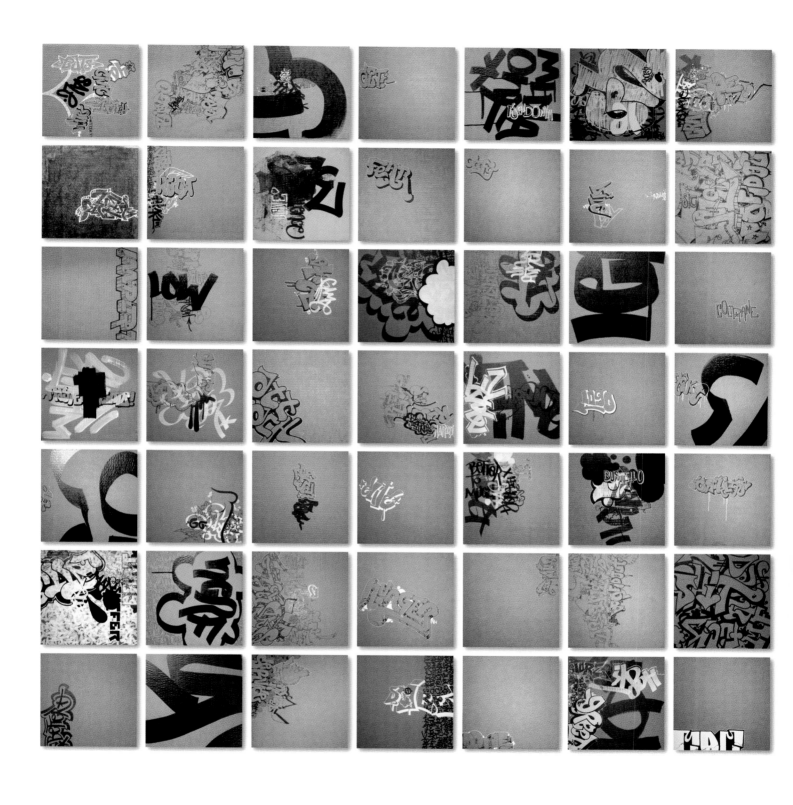

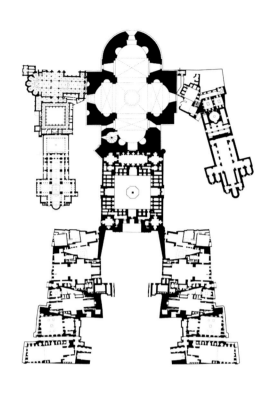

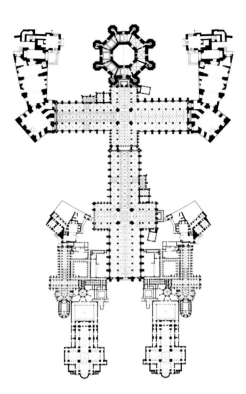

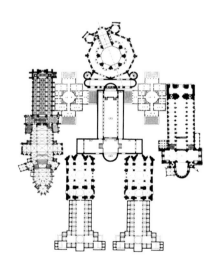

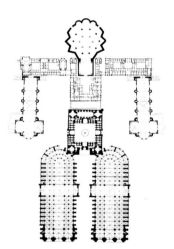

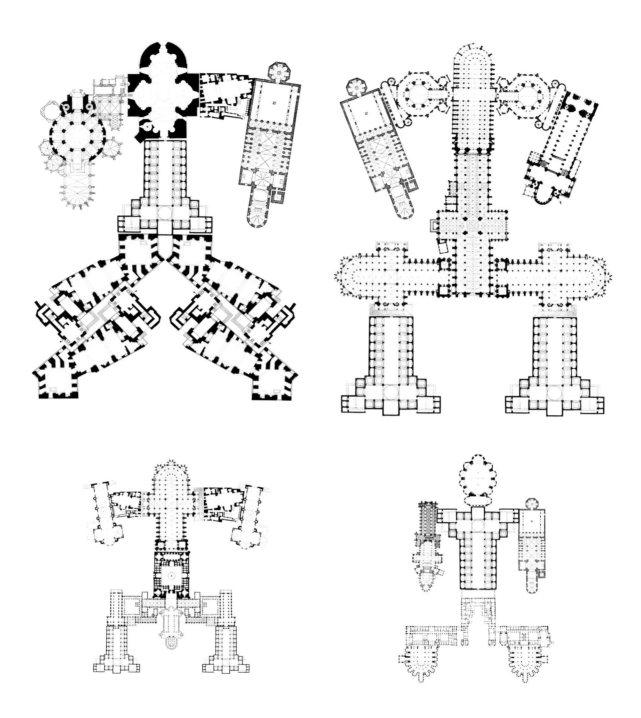

Black Steel in the Hour of Chaos

I GOT A LETTER FROM THE GOVERNMENT THE OTHER DAY I OPENED AND READ IT IT SAID THEY WERE SUCKERS THEY WANTED ME FOR THEIR ARMY OR WHATEVER PICTURE ME GIVEN' A DAMN - I SAID NEVER HERE IS A LAND THAT NEVER GAVE A DAMN ABOUT A BROTHER LIKE ME AND MYSELF BECAUSE THEY NEVER DID I WASN'T WIT' IT, BUT JUST THAT ... OK ... ED TO ... THE SUCKERS HAD AUTHORITY COLD SWEATIN' AS I DWELL IN MY CELL ... ... SITTIN' IN THE STATE PEN I GOTTA GET OUT - BUT THAT THOUGHT WAS THOUGHT BEFORE I CONTEMPLATED A PLAN ON THE CELL FLOOR I'M NOT A FUGITIVE ON THE RUN BUT A BROTHER ... BEGUN ... ANOTHER ONE PUBLIC ENEMY SERVIN' TIME - THEY DREW THE LINE Y'ALL TO CRI ... ... - NEVER THE LESS THEY COULD NOT UNDERSTAND THAT I'M A BLACK MA ... COULD ... ... A VETE ... ... STRENGTH, THE SITUATION'S UNREAL I GOT A RAW DEAL, SO I ... ... STEEL ...
THEY GOT ME ROTTIN' IN ... ... OWED THE SAME TIME THEY'RE THROWIN' 4 OF US ... ... OT US LIVIN' IS HIS HELL YOU HAVE ... ... OF S ... ... WARM OF DEVILS STRAIGHT UP - WOR ... ... VEL THE REASONS ARE SEVERAL ... ... EDERAL HERE IS MY PLAN ANYWA ... ... TO AND NEVER DID ... ... BLOCK AND LOCKED ... ... 'CAN ... ... OSE AND TO THEM ... ... O-AHEAD ON THE ...

YOU KNOW ... ... ON ... CY ... ... WHAT I SAID SO AND EVERYMAN ... ... LE ... WAS DESERVED TO UNDERSTAND MY DE ... NIN' - I W ... ... THE GO ... LUS THE WARDEN TO KNOW THAT I WAS IN ... ENT - BECAU ... IM ... TANT ... OING ... THREAT YO ... IT'S FUCKIN' UP THE GOVERNMENT MY PLAN SA ... TO GET ... ND BRE ... TH JUS ... SH OLIVER'S NECK I HAD TO GET OFF - MY BOYS H ... ... N CHEC ... THEY COULDN'T DO NUTH ... FORCE TO INSTIGATE A PRISON RIOT THIS IS ... E SO ... OOK ... ACK INSIDE TIME TO CUT THE LEASH FRE ... ... GE ... THE ... ... NO ... IT WE OUGHT TO PUT THEIR HEAD OUT BUT I'LL ... ... MA CHANCE, CA ... CIVILIZE ... IS FOR A ... REST OF THE WORLD, THEY CAN'T REALIZE A CELL IS HE ... ... EL SO I ... BETWEE ... ... ME THINKIN' LIKE AN ANIMAL GOT A WOMAN C-O TO CALL ME A ... OPTER SHE TRIED TO GET AWAY, AND I POPPED HER TWICE, RIGHT NOW WHO WANNA GET NICE? I HAD 6 C-O ... ... - CALL ME DELIRIOUS BUT I'M STILL A CA ... INET GOTTA RAP ... THIS TIME ... ... GOT THE STEEL IN MY RIGHT HAND NOW I'M LOOKIN' FOR THE FENCE ...

I VENTURED INTO THE COURTYARD ... ... SED, BATTERED, AND SCARRED BUT HARD GOIN' OUT WITH A BANG REA ... ... OM THE SKY AND FROM THE TOWER SHOTS RANG OUT A HIGH NUMBER ... ... CLOSE FIGURE I TRIGGER MY STEEL STAND AND HOLD MY POST THIS IS W ... ... HINE IF I COME OUT ALIVE AND THEN THEY WON'T - COME CLEAN AND THEN I THREW UP ... ... STEEL BULLETS - FLEW UP BLEW UP, WHO SHOT ... WHAT, WHO, THE BAZOOKA WAS WHO AND TO MY ... UE, IT WAS THE S1WS SECURED MY GETAWAY, SO I JUST GOTAWAY THE JOINT BROKE, FROM THE BLACK ... MOKE THEN THEY SAW IT WAS ROUGHER THAN THE AVERAGE BLUFFER 'CAUSE THE STEEL WAS BLACK, THE ATTITUDE EXACT NOW THE CHASE IS ON TELLIN' YOU TO C'MON 53 BROTHERS ON THE RUN, AND WE ARE GONE

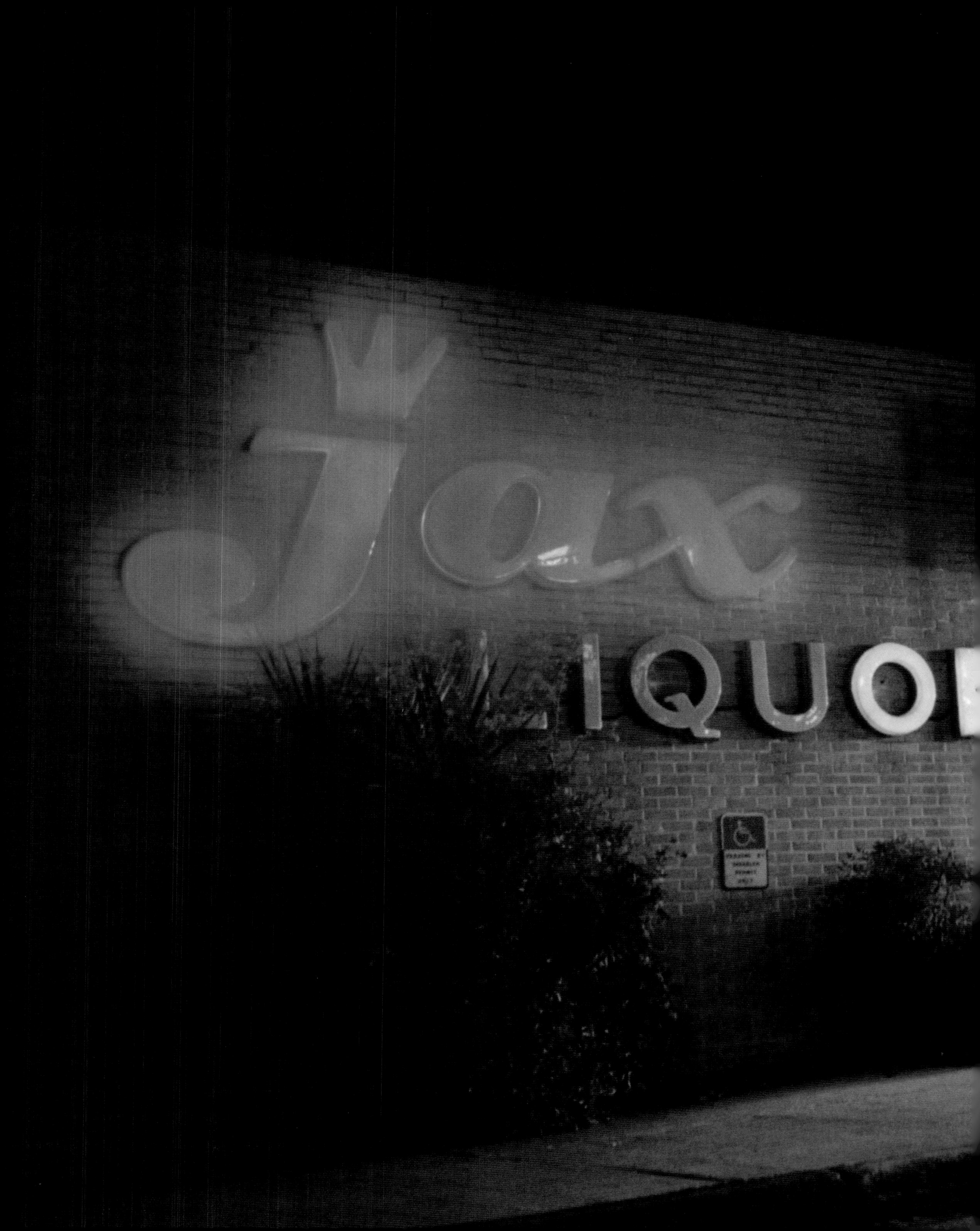
Jax
IQUO

3rd grade

"What I'd Like To Happen For"

"Summer Vacation"

First of all I'm going to Tom's
house and spend the night for one
month, and then we'll go to Michael Jackson's
house and make our eyes like saucers. Next
we'll go to Lebanon, I'll fight but Tom
will have feet of clay ofcourse and
my blood will be boiling and Tom will
be sitting there with stupid clay feet
next will go to china and our hands
will be flying making dresses for
chinese dancers. Then we'll go to
Egypt and go to my cousin's house.
But Tom wouldn't know what kind of
butterflies were in his stomach not me
because I was used it and because
my mind is like a sponge.

MIXED METAL

VANGAURDS OF NEW LEISURE

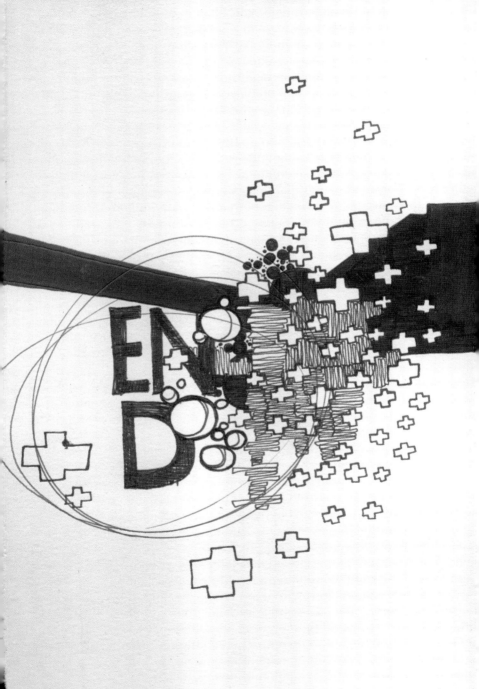

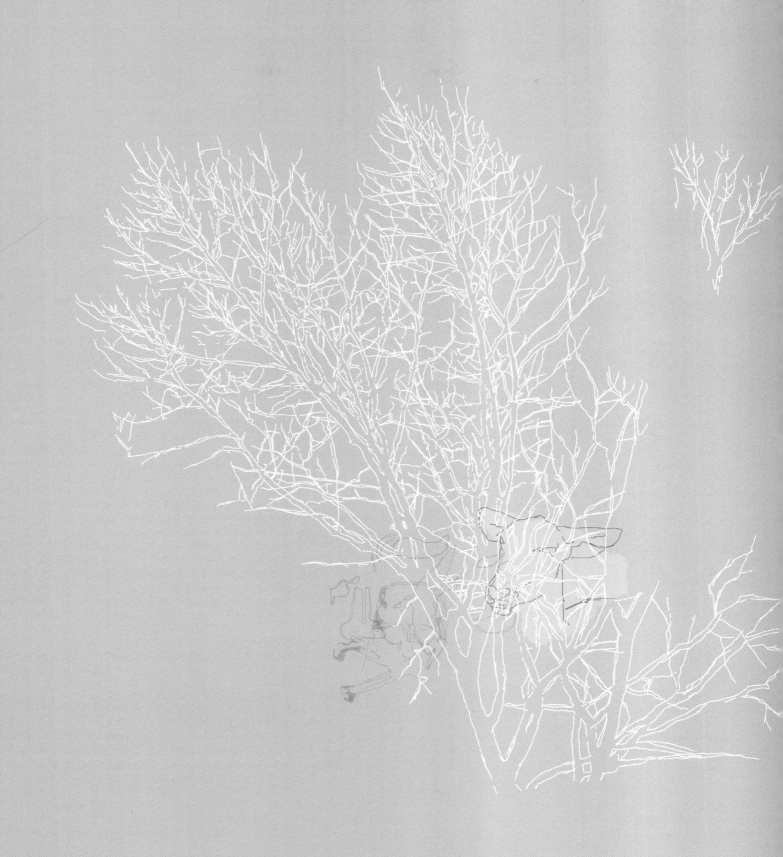

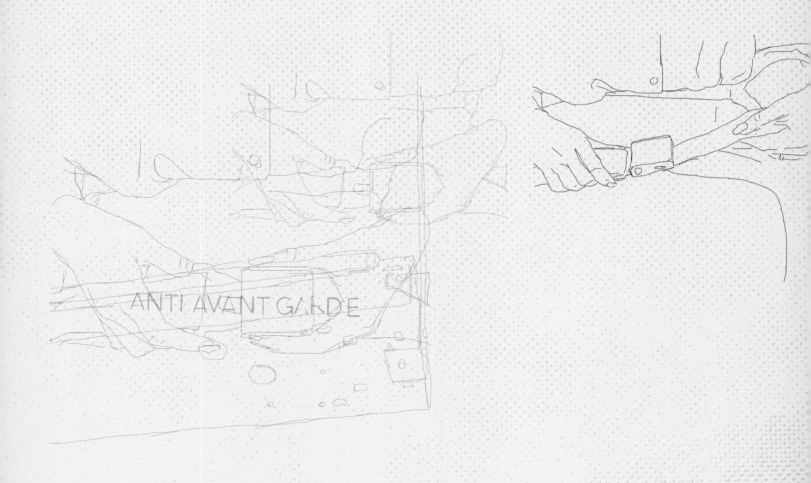

ANTI AVANT GARDE

for Judy Lynn Brown

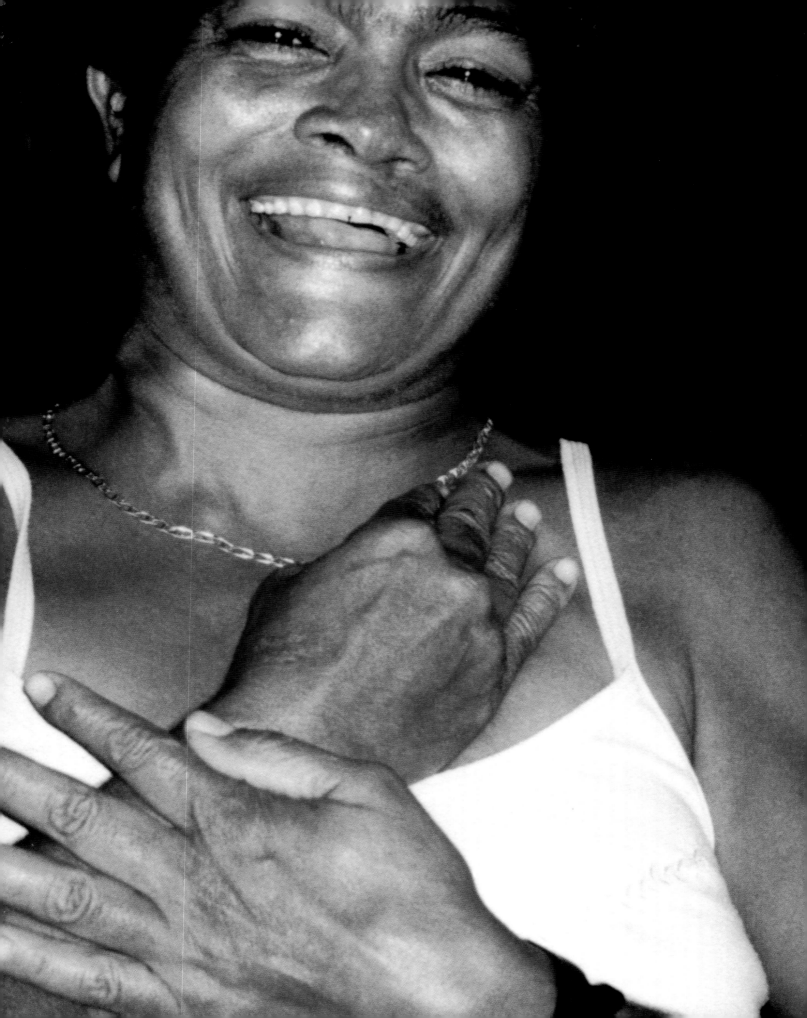

David would like to thank: Mom and Dad thank you for everything I have, Kathleen for letting me beat you up all my life, and all of my beautiful friends: Darrin Mitchell, Christopher Garrett, Chad Werner, Todd Rivera, Touchdown, Jones, Tetsuo!!, H-bomb, Johnny Shillereff, Heather Lewis, Chris and Trey, Elaine, BK (A.E.C.), RVU III, John Dupree, Granto, Yuko Maezawa, Camden and Whit, Jennifer Coffey, Leslie Hard, Mike and Cheryle, Jody, Jen Johnson, Lian and Alona, Jen Hung, Jen Leong, Jessika, Sweet B!, Daniel P., Low down dirty LO, Swanette, Simo, Malinda, Horsie, Cameron Martin, Manny Boy.

Derek would like to thank: First and foremost my family, Dogulas Anderson School of the Arts, Bill Bartlett III, Boo, Jeremiah Brown, Richard & Jackie Cornatzer, Ryan Coleman, Indira Cruz, DremOne TLM, Rayburn Edwards, Kenny Thomas, Antar Fierce, Eric Gilliard, Jose Gomez, Andy Howell, Anthony Hakmati, Steve Kirkland, Joanna Lemmon, Jerry & Debbora Lerner, Jolinda Dian Paul, Patty Powers, Mary Eadon Robinson, JazOne, Dr. Dax, Carolyn Walters.

Peter would like to thank: My family (Jack, Risa and Marge) for putting up with my teenage fanzine habit, Carolina Chaves for encouragement and love, George Estrada and Charlie Becker for getting me into what we do, Scott Herren for pushing and of course Derek, Randall, Sadek and David for putting up with me on a daily basis.

Randall would like to thank: Derek for starting all of this with me what seems like three lifetimes ago. Peter, David and Sadek for joining in the fray and bringing so much. My mom, dad and family for raising me the way that you did. Jerry and Debbora Lerner for all the support and the Quadra. Christopher, my brother. Judy Brown, i love you.

Sadek would like to thank: First and foremost my parents [and family] for their undying love and support. Rick Moore, Margot Jacobs, David Daniell, Jason Seebode, Joanna Lemmon, Jon Philpot, James Elliot, Claudia Deheza, Bryan Collins, Brett Erickson, Jenny Smith, Jack Tiranasar, Adam Wills, Jason Revel, Kelly Clark, and all the others who have shared their inspiration and support along the way.

We would all like to thank: Larry Jens Anderson, The City of Atlanta, Aurora Coffee, Kristin Blandford, Bryan and Brett, Bruce Bohannon, Judy Brown, Louis Ceruzzi, George Chang, Edward Booth-Clibborn, Marcia Cohen, Bryan Collins, Jordan Crane, Indira Cruz, Criminal Records, Brian Donelly, Kenny Dread, John Esguerra, Jody Fausett, Elaine Gardner, Marc-Alan Gray, Mike Hirsch, Scott Herren, Andy Howell, John Hughes III, Karen Ingram, Una Kim, Design is Kinky, David Kinsey, Mike Long, Craig Metzger, David Naugle, KeenOne, JazOne, ChaseOnly, Michael Paine, Yvette and Darrin Prindle, Issac Ramos, John Robinson, Stefan and Andrea Rosso, Bridget Russo, Jonathan B. Schafrann, Jennifer Smith, Scott Andrew Snyder, Mike Steed, Steve and Michelle, Kip Thomas, Jack Tiranasar, Todd Triplet, Ben Velez, Shalini Vora, Norman Wagner, Helen Walters, Jamie Ward, Peter Wong, Stanley Yorker.